The New HR

■ SMART STRATEGIES SERIES ■

The New HR

Dr. Jonathan Smilansky

Senior Vice-President of Human Resources
PolyGram International

INTERNATIONAL THOMSON BUSINESS PRESS
I(T)P® **An International Thomson Publishing Company**

London ● Bonn ● Boston ● Johannesburg ● Madrid ● Melbourne ● Mexico City ● New York ● Paris
Singapore ● Tokyo ● Toronto ● Albany, NY ● Belmont, CA ● Cincinnati, OH ● Detroit, MI

The New HR

Copyright ©1997 J. Smilansky

First published by International Thomson Business Press

 A division of International Thomson Publishing Inc.
The ITP logo is a trademark under licence

British Library Cataloguing-in-Publication Data
A catalogue record for this book is available from the British Library

First edition 1997
Reprinted 1997

Typeset by Laserscript Ltd, Mitcham, Surrey
Printed in Croatia

ISBN 1-86152-112-X

International Thomson Business Press
Berkshire House
168–173 High Holborn
London WC1V 7AA
UK

International Thomson Business Press
20 Park Plaza
13th Floor
Boston MA 02116
USA

http://www.itbp.com

Contents

Acknowledgements

I would not have been able to write this book without the help of many colleagues. First were all those involved in the work of the Personnel Standards Lead Body who contributed directly and indirectly to the concepts and data presented here. Especially I should like to thank Dr. Tina Townsend who chaired the working sessions and created the vision of what could be achieved. Also Dr. Karen Moloney from Moloney & Geally and Judy Whittaker from the Institute of Personnel and Development with whom I worked very closely on the development of the model of HR services, the development of Standards and the structure of qualifications.

My thinking about the strategic role of the HR function and how it can be improved has been developed together with many colleagues inside organizations and in consultancies. It would be very difficult to thank everyone but I was especially grateful for the opportunity to work and to think together with Alan Little, Avivit Shpizisen, Brian Sullivan, Avi Engel, Clinton Wingrove, David Owen and John Stokes.

I am also extremely thankful to Pilat (UK) Ltd., which provided me with the opportunity to manage the project with the Personnel Standards Lead Body and enabled me to do much of the work described in this book.

Finally, I am forever indebted to Errica Moustaki and Dr. Anton Obholzer who taught me everything I know about resistance to change; and to my father who taught me how to ask the truly important questions.

Introduction

'

The ideas presented in this book have come about as a result of my experience in a number of work settings. I began as a general manager in Visa International responsible for internal services including HR management, finance, facilities, management information services and Total Quality Management. This combined role made it clear, that from an integrated corporate perspective, it is essential to ensure that all staff functions can specify their contribution, or added value, to the achievement of the overall business strategy. The combination of the implementation of Total Quality Management and the need to cut costs dramatically in order to improve competitive advantage, provided a unique opportunity to develop a variety of improvement processes across various staff functions. By using the work of others and engaging internal teams, we were able to clarify where we were working effectively and where large-scale changes of priorities as well as service improvements within existing priority areas had to be achieved.

Through my consultancy experience, first as a partner in Hay Management Consultants and then as a director of Pilat (UK) Limited, I have worked with many clients to examine the effectiveness of their Human Resource (HR) services. While in the early 1980s many Personnel functions were examining new ideas about the move to more advanced HR management approaches, in the last few years the focus has shifted radically towards the need to justify direct contribution to the achievement of strategic business aims.

During 1993 and 1994 I led the development work for the Personnel Standards Lead Body which involved representatives of leading UK organizations in an effort to establish best practice across the field, as a basis for developing qualifications at all levels of practice. (All the information collected for the Personnel Standards Lead Body is Crown Copyright and therefore available freely to the public on request. It is published here with the permission of the Department of Employment, which funded the work).

This project involved research with very large benchmark samples, across public and private sector organizations. It focused on the perceptions of Personnel practitioners and line managers about what is more or less important and how well service is being delivered. This unique database provides probably one of the largest samples of information available anywhere in the world about current practice within the HR management field.

My experience as the senior vice-president, Human Resources at Forte Hotels and now at Polygram International provided me with exceptional opportunities to put research findings and my experience as a consultant into practice. By focusing the HR function on improving its strategic contribution to the business, it is clear that we can influence overall business performance, as described here.

The key messages of the book are presented through the following chapters:

In Chapter One we explore why it is important to improve the delivery of HR services. It includes a brief review of the nature of organizational change resulting from internal and external pressures that have been experienced in the private and public sectors. We look at the impact of this change on the nature of the HR function within organizations and discuss how the need for change brought about increased pressure to justify business contribution given the overhead nature of HR services. The need to improve is also examined in the light of Total Quality Management (TQM) approaches that have expanded across organizational boundaries and entered into staff functions. The chapter concludes with an improvement model that encompasses the approaches discussed in the rest of the book.

The first of these approaches is presented in Chapter Two, which deals with self-assessment techniques. This chapter describes a process through which HR practitioners can assess where they are stronger and weaker in providing services to the organization and how they can go about setting priorities for improvement.

Chapter Three focuses on collecting feedback from internal customers. Specific data collection methods are provided in order to examine what line managers think of the variety of services that HR practitioners provide for improving management effectiveness in their organization.

Chapters Two and Three also include large-scale benchmark data that has been collected as part of the Personnel Standards Lead Body's work. This data provides input from nearly a thousand public and private sector organizations where the heads of HR departments describe the relative importance of a range of services they deliver internally and rate the effectiveness of their own function in providing these services. The information from these organizations makes it possible for you to collect data within your own setting using the same questionnaire and to compare the perceptions of your own function's strengths and weaknesses with those of other functions. Chapter Three also includes case study information from around 30 blue chip organizations. The HR function in these organizations asked their internal customers, senior and middle managers what they saw as priority areas and how they perceived the effectiveness of service provision. Once again, the information described here enables you to collect data from line managers in your organization and to compare it with the data from the case study organizations. You will then have concrete benchmarks to establish how well you are doing and where there are areas of priority for improving the quality of your services.

Chapter Four focuses on analysing your current HR budget allocation and on analysing how staff spend their time on a range of services. By collecting this data you will be able to identify *de facto* priorities in the services provided by your HR function. You can also use these tools to compare your current activities and resource allocations with your long-term priorities.

Chapter Five focuses on current HR practitioners' range of capabilities in your organization and thereby enables you to relate these capabilities to the priorities established for the function as a whole. Specific self assessment and manager assessment tools are made available for you to gather the information required. By collecting such data you will be able to establish staff training and development needs as well as ascertain areas where you do not have staff with the competence required for effective service delivery.

Chapter Six endeavours to establish an HR strategy to support the overall organizational strategy. The chapter reviews the need to not only improve existing services, but also to be clear about where the organization as a whole is going and how adopting specific organization strategies should drive the nature of services and priorities that the HR function establishes. This chapter focuses on how you can clarify the key elements of the organization's long-term strategy, what an HR strategy would look like and how you can relate the HR function's contribution to the overall effectiveness of the organization. Chapter Six also gives you tools to examine the current services provided by the HR function in your organization in light of its strategy. This will make it possible to set priorities and to crystallize what is important in order to provide added value to the achievement of the organization's long-term aims.

Chapter Seven moves into more detailed planning by describing the process for establishing targets for HR service delivery. Following a discussion on the importance of target setting as a basis for improvement, this chapter describes how to set targets and how to distinguish between outcome and milestone targets in hard and soft areas. The chapter also provides examples of targets for the different areas of HR service delivery. Target setting is viewed as an interactive process involving internal customers as well as having a strategic focus in order to ensure long-term added value.

Chapter Eight focuses on implementing functional change following the use of the tools and processes described in the book. Improving your HR function's effectiveness is going to require a process of change, both for your own team as well as in the relationships between yourselves and your internal customers. The chapter discusses the nature of change, why change is a difficult process and how various defensive processes arise in the organization against change. The discussion shows you how to deal with your own team to ensure that everyone participates in the diagnosis of strengths and weaknesses and comes up with priorities and action plans for improving effectiveness.

This chapter also considers communication to your internal customers. It discusses the need to admit service delivery problems, how to involve customers in setting priorities and how to create an atmosphere of trust in which success is celebrated and systematic. Continuous improvement processes are also considered.

The book concludes with an appendix of all the data collection and analysis tools presented in the above chapters. You are encouraged to use them towards improving the strategic contribution of HR in your organization.

CHAPTER ONE

The need for change in Human Resources

This chapter summarizes the key changes that during the last few years have influenced the nature of services provided by the HR function. Data from a large-scale occupational survey conducted by the Personnel Standards Lead Body quantifies the prevalence of these changes across public and private sector organizations in the UK.

In working with a large number of organizations across the UK, it is clear that everyone is experiencing large-scale changes. Some managers feel that these changes will eventually subside, when it will be possible to take stock and start to crystallize the new situation into a more effective permanent state of business activity. In reality, however, organizational change has become a permanent state of affairs. Rapid changes in technology, the emergence of new competitive organizations, the disbanding of legal/protective boundaries around many public sector organizations, have all resulted in massive changes. The nature of business processes, the markets in which organizations are operating, the structures used and typically also the number and type of people who are involved in delivering the business strategy are in a constant state of flux.

The HR management function has not escaped these changes. Organizations are increasingly having to cut overhead costs, not only by reducing labour overall but also by reducing radically the ratio between staff and line jobs. Initially, these pressures were accommodated by reducing at the periphery of service delivery. But with time the size of the required reduction pushed many organizations towards a basic review of the services provided by the HR management function. This review has tended, in many organizations, to result in a change of focus from a more administrative, service delivery approach provided by a large number of relatively junior practitioners, to a more strategic consultancy service, in which the HR function provides guidance and advice to line management.

The Personnel administration aspects of the work are now often being done by the supervisors and managers themselves, or in many cases, eliminated altogether by reducing paperwork and the need for written authorization.

A number of other developments in the last few years have contributed to a change in the nature of the services provided by the HR function. Concepts such as decentralization, delayering and empowerment have increased the HR management responsibility of line managers, who are actually engaged day to day in service provision with their staff. These processes resulted in a gradual change in the power relationships within organizations. The power of headquarters functions in the staff areas has been reduced relative to the power of the senior management on the operational side.

Another key change is in the nature of the labour market. The reduction in the power of collective bargaining altered the HR management function's role as a key player for ensuring acceptable industrial relations. In the past it was possible for many HR practitioners to develop a large power base within the organization, thus justifying a need to audit and pre-approve any action by line managers through the fear that local employee resistance might become the catalyst for large-scale business disruption. As the likelihood of this decreased, HR practitioners at head office could no longer justify the need for strict controls over line managers' activities in their organizations. The fact that, at the same time, the overall number of people being recruited into most organizations was dropping significantly also meant that the traditional HR focus on recruitment became a much smaller requirement. Therefore HR practitioners had to change their focus by providing new added value services that line managers would feel the need for. The function could no longer provide administrative and control functions only, which in many cases were viewed by line managers as preventing them from doing what they thought was appropriate from their local business perspective.

This shift in focus meant that it was no longer clear why an organization needed an HR management department unless they could clearly provide a level of expertise not available to the typical line manager. This shift meant that HR practitioners had to increase their own level of expertise or, alternatively, more administratively-oriented junior practitioners had to be replaced with more highly experienced professionals. These staff had to have a level of expertise that line managers would perceive as adding value to their own decision-making processes.

Another influence on the requirements for change within the HR function was the gradual implementation of Total Quality Management (TQM) techniques. Originally TQM tended to be applied in the operational functions of the manufacturing sector. These initiatives gradually moved to the service industry but only recently has TQM been applied to staff functions. This new focus meant that staff had to view their customers as being more than merely a vague corporate entity for which they are the guardian. Line managers became the key clients, requiring services from the HR function in order to manage their relationship with the external environment more effectively. On the positive side, of all the staff functions, HR has tended to take a lead in attempting to adopt TQM processes. One very rarely hears of marketing or finance adopting a client-oriented service level agreement to ensure their effectiveness. In many organizations the HR function gradually took control of implementing TQM, or other service quality improvement processes; it is becoming clear that the key success factor is a basic attitude change enabling all levels in the organization to focus on continuous improvement processes by using concrete performance-related information. Leading TQM activities across the business meant that HR itself also had to focus internally by applying the same concepts to the way they were providing services to their internal customers.

Thus the HR function is going through major structural and process changes. The need to improve, therefore, results from the comparison between the current state of affairs in most organizations and a shared view of what could be achieved if everyone acknowledged the need to add value to the business and the concept of continuous improvement built into TQM approaches.

Some of these changes can be seen through a more quantitative view of the pressures experienced in the HR function as provided by a recent large-scale occupational survey conducted by the Personnel Standards Lead Body (1994).

Data was collected from a large national sample of public and private sector organizations, of various sizes, in order to understand how HR practitioners view the changes that have occurred in their function. Respondents were asked to describe, among other things, their main area of activity (generalists or specialists) and what they saw as the main changes in the HR function within their organization. All questions were pilot tested in order to ensure understanding. The final version of the questionnaire was sent to the head of the HR function in approximately 3,000 organizations. They were asked to respond themselves and to give another copy of the questionnaire to a younger member of their staff. Fifteen hundred completed questionnaires were returned, representing about half senior and half more junior practitioners.The key findings are summarized overleaf.

In both the public and private sectors the data in Figures 1.1 and 1.2 shows that respondents are distributed across a range of areas of specialization with a very significant number of practitioners (about two-thirds) who describe themselves as generalists.

FIGURE 1.1 Respondents' main area of activity – public sector

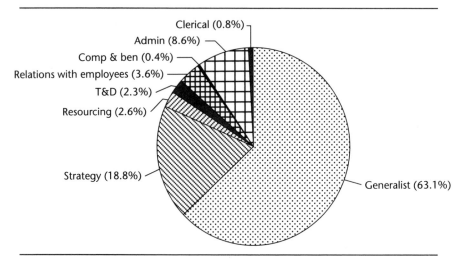

FIGURE 1.2 Respondents' main area of activity – private sector

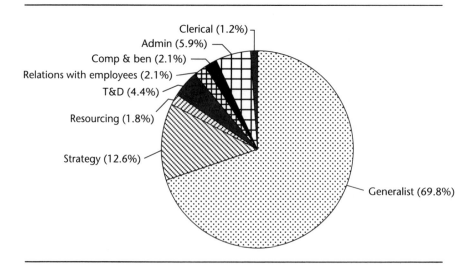

Respondents were asked to rate to what extent a number of potential changes to the HR function applied to their organization, now or in the near future.

There were only small differences between the public and private sector respondents' perception of the key changes in the function within their organization.

Of the list of changes provided in the questionnaire, the four which were listed as predominant in both sectors were (Figures 1.3 and 1.4):

- 'The need for increased contribution of Personnel to business performance' (item 5)

- 'An increased need to justify Personnel's position' (item 7)

- 'More devolution of Personnel functions to the Line' (item 1)

- And to some degree, in the public sector, an expectation in the near future for 'More specialist expertise in the Personnel function' (item 4).

In all these items respondents indicated that they expect the trend to increase in the near future.

This quantitative data from the occupational survey conducted by the Personnel Standards Lead Body (1994) illustrates the increased pressures on HR functions to justify their contribution to the current and future success of the organization.

But increased pressure does not necessarily result in improving functional performance. To improve the effectiveness of the HR function we need to be clear about how we can increase our value added to the organization.

We need various types of information to ascertain the gap between what we could and what we actually deliver. First, we need to be clear about the range of HR management services that can be provided. This will enable us to clarify our own perceptions about the relative importance of each service to current and future organizational success. It will also enable us to describe where we feel we are delivering a more or a less effective service.

Second, this map of potential services can be used to assess our internal clients' perspectives of what is important for organizational success and how capable we are in delivering an effective service in each area.

Third, we can use this map of services to examine our budget for staff and other resources and, thereby, review the degree to which we put our money 'where our mouth is' by comparing budgets to expressed service priorities. In this category of information we can analyse more

FIGURE 1.3 Personnel Standards Lead Body – Occupational Survey, 1994: changes in the Personnel profession, public sector

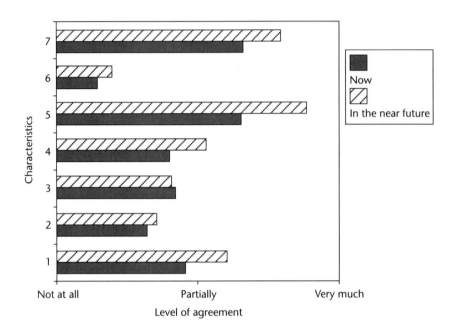

1 **Devolved Personnel function to the line**
2 **Reduced number of staff in Personnel**
3 **More generalists in Personnel function**
4 **More specialist expertise in Personnel function**
5 **Increased contribution to business performance**
6 **Transfer of some functions from the line to specialist personnel**
7 **Increased need to justify Personnel's position**

deeply the effectiveness of resource allocation by analysing activity and comparing where the function spends most of its time against stated organizational priorities.

Fourth, we can review the existing 'competence pool' within the HR function. This information (using self and boss assessment) will enable us to compare what we, as a team, can do in the light of our expressed priorities.

Finally, we can examine the longer-term business strategy and analyse, at a more conceptual level, the potential contribution of the HR

FIGURE 1.4   Personnel Standards Lead Body – Occupational Survey, 1994: changes in the Personnel profession, private sector

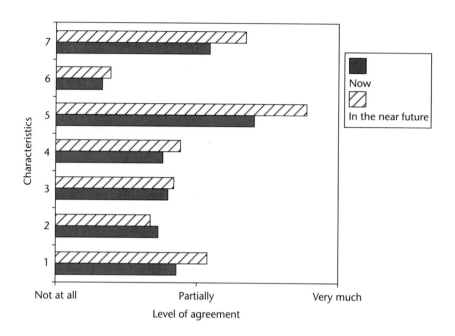

1 **Devolved Personnel function to the line**
2 **Reduced number of staff in Personnel**
3 **More generalists in Personnel function**
4 **More specialist expertise in Personnel function**
5 **Increased contribution to business performance**
6 **Transfer of some functions from the line to specialist personnel**
7 **Increased need to justify Personnel's position**

function to its achievement. In some organizations the long-term strategy will require fundamental changes to key business processes. In such cases improving the effectiveness of current HR services or satisfying current line management requests may not provide the foundation for the required long-term changes.

These five data sources will enable us to compare current and future organizational priorities with the capability of our HR function. This comparison forms the basis for effective functional strategy, organization and work processes that will guide our improvement actions. The rationale, process and tools required to collect these five types of information are provided in the following chapters, together with illustrative case study results. The final chapters describe how to integrate the data as a basis for functional improvement.

The model in Figure 1.5 is a graphic illustration of the improvement process that provides the outline for this book.

FIGURE 1.5   A model of the improvement process

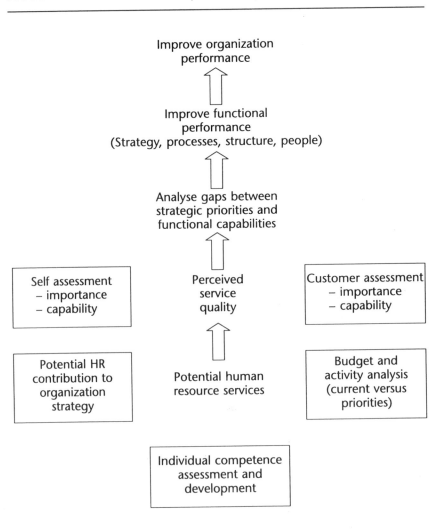

CHAPTER TWO

Self-assessment

This chapter describes the range of services that can be provided by an HR department within an organization and a self-assessment tool to enable HR practitioners to compare the relative importance they attribute to these services and their capability to deliver them effectively. This information is supported by data collected from 978 heads of Human Resources in public and private sector organizations who used this self-assessment tool to rate services provided in their own settings. You can use this benchmark data to compare with self-assessment data within your own organization.

The first step towards improving your organization's HR function is to set priorities. You and your staff should begin with a systematic self-assessment to decide what services are important for the organization's long-term success. This should also reveal any major problems in service delivery, that if improved, can increase the overall added value of the HR function.

The first step in self diagnosis is to examine the services which are and could be provided by your HR department. The work of the Personnel Standards Lead Body is exceptionally relevant here. During 1994 the Personnel Standards Lead Body held meetings with individual HR directors of leading organizations and group meetings with many experienced senior practitioners in the field. The purpose of these meetings was to develop a clear map of the function as it is delivered in large and small organizations within the private and public sector. We started to define the key component of HR by stating what we see as the overall purpose of the HR function. This was seen as aiming:

To enable management to enhance the individual and collective contribution of people to the short- and long-term success of the enterprise.

To achieve this key purpose the HR department provides a wide range of internal services. As a result of consultation with practitioners across a large number of organizations, we have grouped these services into the following five clusters:

Cluster A is **strategy and organization**. Includes the contribution of HR practitioners to the development and review of the organization's strategy, the development and review of organization structures and work processes to improve effectiveness as well as the review and improvement of organization culture and values to ensure that they support the long-term strategy.

Cluster B is **resourcing**. It includes developing and maintaining resourcing strategy and plans to consider the strategic needs of the organization, recruiting new people, deploying people effectively within the organization, releasing employees from the organization, and using contracted or temporary employees as part of the work force.

Cluster C is **development**. It includes developing and maintaining strategy and plans to enhance individuals' and groups' performance in order to improve the organization's long-term competitive positioning; establishing performance planning and review processes; promoting training to improve individuals' capacity to perform; promoting long-term individual development; and promoting team development.

Cluster D focuses on services in the area of **reward management**. It includes developing and maintaining total remuneration strategy and plans; establishing levels of remuneration for jobs and people; developing and managing effective employee benefits and expenses and finally paying employees.

The last cluster of HR services, E, focuses on issues around **relations with employees**. This includes both organizational development type services such as developing and maintaining strategy and plans for all employee relations activities; ensuring employees' commitment in times of change; and promoting effective internal communication to support the achievement of the organization's strategy. This cluster also includes more traditional industrial relations type services such as employee support services (counselling and welfare); ensuring compliance with organization policy and legal requirements; negotiation and consultation with groups and individuals; handling grievance and discipline; health and safety; and promoting equal opportunities.

The five clusters of services described above are illustrated in Figure 2.1, which represents the integrated nature of HR services and includes three key parts. First, the pyramid structure in the middle represents the range of internal services provided by the HR function. These fall into the five clusters described earlier. Second, the ribbon wrapped around the pyramid represents

FIGURE 2.1   The five clusters of services

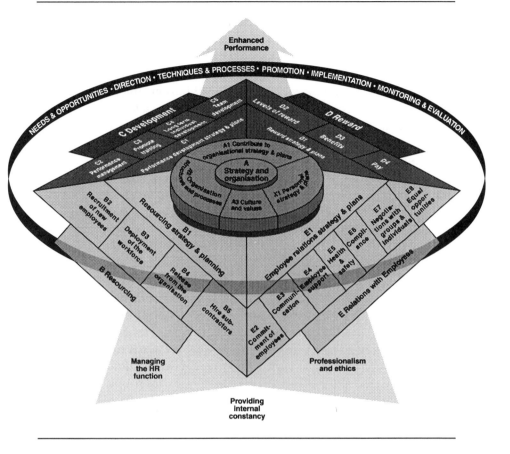

the work process necessary to deliver effective service in each area. Finally, the bottom represents additional key components including management of the HR team itself, enabling line managers to carry out HR management activities themselves and the professionalism and ethics required of an effective practitioner.

We first review the range of services described in the pyramid. The organization and strategic elements of the HR function are on top of the pyramid to illustrate that they drive the provision of other services throughout the organization. Beneath this are the four additional service clusters: resourcing, development, reward and relations with employees.

The first element in each cluster of services always focuses on the development of a strategy and of plans to provide all services in the given area. This element of service management is lacking in a number of organizations. There was, however, wide consensus among senior practitioners throughout the consultation process about the importance of strategic components for all HR services to ensure that priorities are established and that added value is clearly demonstrated to the organization as a whole.

In addition to the provision of the specific services described above, the extensive consultation process suggested that the entire range of HR services should include within it a sequence of work processes, or activities that form the basis for the effective provision of any service. More specifically, six work processes identified as critical are included in the ribbon around the pyramid in Figure 2.1:

1   Identifying the *needs* of various internal client groups and the *opportunities* to improve the organization's effectiveness by providing various HR management services.

2   Establishing the *direction* for providing services, including setting objectives for service delivery and internal client understanding of quality standards associated with them.

3   Designing and selecting the best *tools*, *processes* and *systems* for providing state-of-the-art service within each of those areas to meet the objectives set in number two above, and to provide added value to the organization.

4   *Promoting* and *communicating* to internal clients the advantages of the service provided by the HR department so that they can see how these services can be utilized to improve overall organizational effectiveness.

5   *Implementing* a service or setting up new ways of providing HR services to improve performance.

6   *Monitoring* and *evaluating* the HR service provided in relation to its previously-stated objectives, which outline its potential contribution to organization performance.

All the work processes described above are relevant to each one of the services identified earlier, thereby creating a matrix where one can multiply the range of services by the key steps in the work process.

Finally, in addition to providing these HR services and working through the processes above, it is important for the HR department to be managed effectively itself and to enable other people who are not HR practitioners to carry out these functions. Those two additional areas of competence are critical in evaluating the overall effectiveness of the HR department and are therefore listed at the bottom of the pyramid. The need for professionalism and ethics in HR tasks is also illustrated at that point.

A brief self-assessment questionnaire devised to enable HR practitioners to review the range of service provided in their organization in relation to the functional map developed by the Personnel Standards Lead Body is provided here and in the Appendix for your own self-assessment.

THE KEY FUNCTIONS OF PERSONNEL

Listed below are Personnel services grouped under five headings. Under each function we would like you to respond to the following:

- **Importance for the future success of your organization**
  Please circle the number in the column that best reflects the importance of each function to the future success of your organization.
- **Current personnel capability**
  The capability of your Personnel function to deliver each Personnel function effectively.

Please circle the number in the column that best reflects the current capability of your organization to perform this function.

You have the opportunity to comment on your ratings if you wish.

A. Strategy and organization	Importance for future success					Current personnel capability				
	1 Critical 2 Very important 3 Important 4 Helpful 5 Not important					1 Exceptionally good 2 Very good 3 Good 4 Fair 5 Poor				
Contribute to the overall strategy of the organization by providing generalist and specialist information and advice	1	2	3	4	5	1	2	3	4	5
Develop and maintain an appropriate personnel strategy to support the overall strategy of the organization	1	2	3	4	5	1	2	3	4	5
Enable the creation of an organization structure and work processes that maximize the performance of people at work	1	2	3	4	5	1	2	3	4	5
Facilitate the development of organizational values and culture required to support its strategy	1	2	3	4	5	1	2	3	4	5
Facilitate external relations (e.g. purchasers, local authorities, educational institutions)	1	2	3	4	5	1	2	3	4	5

Comments:_____

_____

_____

B. Resourcing	Importance for future success					Current personnel capability				
	1 Critical 2 Very important 3 Important 4 Helpful 5 Not important					1 Exceptionally good 2 Very good 3 Good 4 Fair 5 Poor				
Develop and maintain workforce planning to support current and future requirements	1	2	3	4	5	1	2	3	4	5
Recruit and select people into the organization	1	2	3	4	5	1	2	3	4	5
Optimize the deployment of staff within the organization	1	2	3	4	5	1	2	3	4	5
Identify individual potential to develop and meet future resourcing requirements	1	2	3	4	5	1	2	3	4	5
Release people from the organization (e.g. retirement, redundancy)	1	2	3	4	5	1	2	3	4	5
Engage non-core and temporary staff	1	2	3	4	5	1	2	3	4	5

Comments: _____

_____

_____

C. Development										
Establish and maintain performance management	1	2	3	4	5	1	2	3	4	5
Establish opportunities to enhance individual capability (e.g. training)	1	2	3	4	5	1	2	3	4	5
Promote longer-term individual development processes	1	2	3	4	5	1	2	3	4	5
Facilitate team development processes	1	2	3	4	5	1	2	3	4	5

Comments: _____

_____

_____

D. Compensation and benefits										
Develop and maintain a reward strategy (e.g. pay, benefits)	1	2	3	4	5	1	2	3	4	5
Establish and maintain the criteria for ensuring appropriate level of reward	1	2	3	4	5	1	2	3	4	5
Implement and maintain processes to define employees' terms and conditions of employment	1	2	3	4	5	1	2	3	4	5
Pay contracted employees and others	1	2	3	4	5	1	2	3	4	5
Administer benefits and other payments	1	2	3	4	5	1	2	3	4	5

Comments: _____

_____

_____

E. Relations with employees	Importance for future success					Current personnel capability				
	1 Critical 2 Very important 3 Important 4 Helpful 5 Not important					1 Exceptionally good 2 Very good 3 Good 4 Fair 5 Poor				
Develop and maintain commitment of employees in times of change (e.g. support change programmes)	1	2	3	4	5	1	2	3	4	5
Promote effective communication within the organization	1	2	3	4	5	1	2	3	4	5
Provide counselling and welfare support for the mutual benefit of the organization and the individual	1	2	3	4	5	1	2	3	4	5
Ensure compliance with Personnel-related legislation and internal policies	1	2	3	4	5	1	2	3	4	5
Provide processes for handling grievances and discipline	1	2	3	4	5	1	2	3	4	5
Consult and/or negotiate with employees and/or their representatives to facilitate achievement of organizational goals	1	2	3	4	5	1	2	3	4	5
Promote and ensure equality of opportunity	1	2	3	4	5	1	2	3	4	5
Establish and maintain processes for ensuring health and safety at work	1	2	3	4	5	1	2	3	4	5

Comments:_____

_____

_____

F. Work processes in service delivery

So far we have presented Personnel services and asked you to indicate how effectively they perform in your organization and their importance to the current and future success of your organization.

We would also like your feedback about importance and capability as they apply to the different work processes involved in providing Personnel services.

Assess needs and opportunities to provide and improve Personnel services	1	2	3	4	5	1	2	3	4	5
Design and select techniques and processes for providing Personnel services	1	2	3	4	5	1	2	3	4	5
Market and promote the advantage of utilizing Personnel services	1	2	3	4	5	1	2	3	4	5
Implement and enable others to implement Personnel services	1	2	3	4	5	1	2	3	4	5
Monitor and evaluate the effectiveness of Personnel services	1	2	3	4	5	1	2	3	4	5

Comments:_____

_____

_____

Section A – Strategy and Organization

The self-assessment questionnaire enables you to rate the *importance* of each HR service for the current and future success of your organization and the relative *competence* with which the HR function in your organization provides each service. Through this self-assessment rating you should be able to clarify your own perceptions about priorities. You can also use a wider sample of colleagues within the department to establish a group view about areas of importance and competence and to reach a consensus about what your HR Department does well and what are the key areas for improvement.

In 1994 the Personnel Standards Lead Body surveyed a representative sample of 978 organizations from the public and the private sector, to ascertain the relative importance of various services and the perceived competence with which practitioners think they provide services in each area. The data was collected using the self-assessment questionnaire with the heads of HR departments and represents their own self-assessment. These findings are summarized in Figures 2.2 to 2.7.

FIGURE 2.2   Personnel's view of themselves: Strategy and Organization

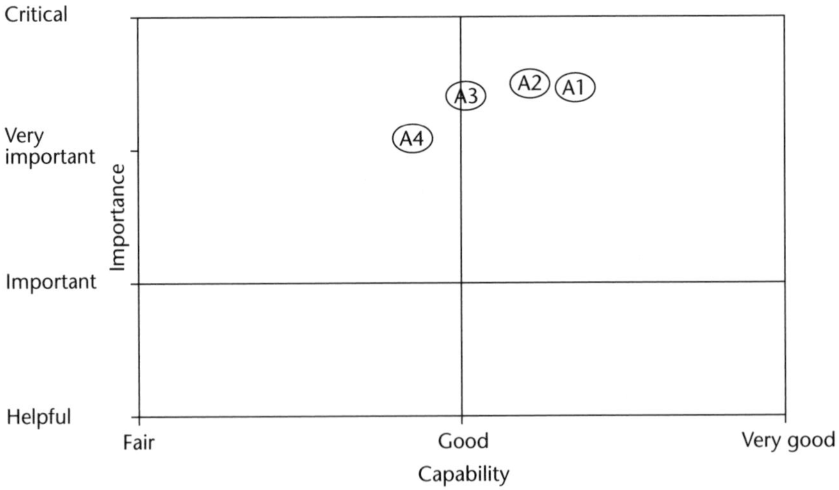

A1= Organization strategy
A2= Personnel strategy
A3= Structure and work processes
A4= Values and culture.

The first set of findings, shown in Figure 2.2, relate to the area of Strategy and Organization. The data is described through a scattergram which plots ratings of perceived importance on one dimension and those of perceived competence on the other dimension. Ideally we would want all services to be in the top-right-hand box where they are perceived to be of high importance to the organization and are being delivered effectively. The main priorities for improvement will be in the top-left-hand box, where services are perceived to be important for the organization's long-term success but are not being delivered in the most effective manner.

The data shows that the heads of HR from this sample perceived all four services in the area of Strategy and Organization to be very important to future organizational success. The first three services (contribute to organization strategy, develop personnel strategy and plans, ensure effective organization structures and work processes) are also perceived to be delivered effectively. Developing an organization culture and values to support the achievement of its strategy is perceived as an area where the quality of service provided by HR practitioners in these organizations should be improved.

Section B – Resourcing

The findings in the area of Resourcing (Figure 2.3) are more complex. The original questionnaire had eight items (after further analysis we reduced the number of items in the next version as provided). Of these services, facilitating the effective use of sub-contractors, temporary and voluntary staff was considered to be of low importance for long-term organizational success (items B6 and BB). This finding is surprising given the increased tendency for organizations to outsource many non-core activities.

The heads of HR in this sample perceived the following services as both important and being delivered effectively:

B1   Developing resourcing plans

B2   External recruitment and selection

B5   Releasing people from the organization.

In contrast, the following services were perceived as equally important for long-term organizational success but that service delivery was less than effective:

FIGURE 2.3 Personnel's view of themselves – Resourcing

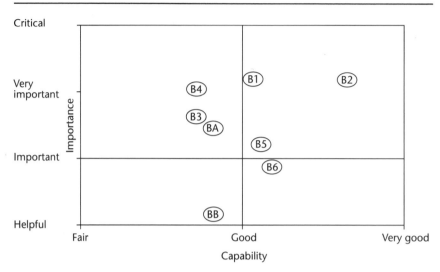

B1 = **Resourcing plans**
B2 = **Recruitment and selection**
B3 = **Internal resourcing**
B4 = **Identifying individual potential**
B5 = **Releasing people**
B6 = **Resourcing sub-contractors and temporary staff**
BA = **Deploying people**
BB = **Engaging voluntary staff.**

B3   Internal resourcing

B4   Identifying individual potential

BA   Deploying people effectively.

Section C – Development

The heads of HR were quite negative when rating development services (Figure 2.4). All three services included in the questionnaire used for that survey were rated as very important for long-term organization success. But, at the same time, the perceptions of this very large sample of respondents was that none of these services was currently delivered effectively. There were variations in ratings across this sample but the overall average pinpoints this area as a key priority for improvement.

FIGURE 2.4 Personnel's view of themselves – Enhance individual and group performance

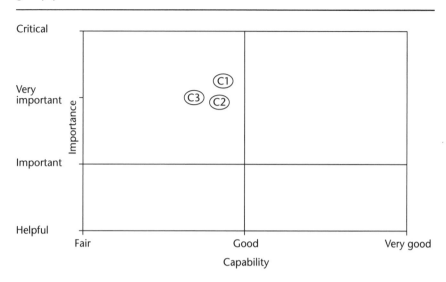

C1= **Performance management**
C2= **Enhance individual capabilities through training**
C3= **Long-term individual development.**

Section D – Reward Management

There is much more of a spread in the findings on services in the area of Reward Management (Figure 2.5). All such services were rated by the respondents as very important to long-term organizational success. Three were also perceived to be delivered effectively, including specifying terms and conditions of employment (D3), paying employees (D4) and administering benefits (D5). The more strategic services were perceived to be delivered less effectively. These include the development of a reward strategy to support the organization's business needs (D1) and the development of effective criteria for providing reward (D2).

Section E – Relations with Employees

The fifth area of HR service focuses on Relations with Employees (Figure 2.6). Most of these services (other than E3 – Counselling and Welfare)

FIGURE 2.5   Personnel's view of themselves – Compensation and Benefits

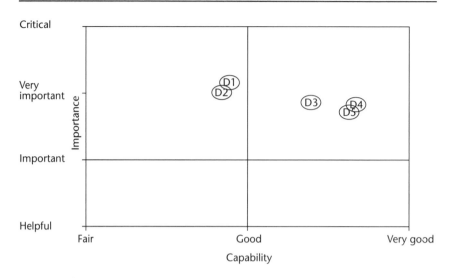

D1= **Developing a reward strategy**
D2= **Establishing criteria for reward**
D3= **Agreeing terms and conditions of employment**
D4= **Paying employees**
D5= **Administering benefits.**

were rated by the 978 heads of HR as very important to long-term organizational success. There were, however, variations in respondents' perceptions about the quality of services provided in each. The more traditional industrial relation services were perceived as being provided effectively. These include:

E4   Compliance with organization policy and legal requirements

E5   Handling grievance and discipline

E6   Consultation and negotiation with individuals and groups

E7   Ensuring equal opportunities

E8   Health and safety at work.

The services in the area of Organization Development (i.e. ensuring employees' commitment in time of change; and facilitating effective internal communications) were perceived to be more problematic in service quality.

FIGURE 2.6   Personnel's view of themselves – Relations with Employees

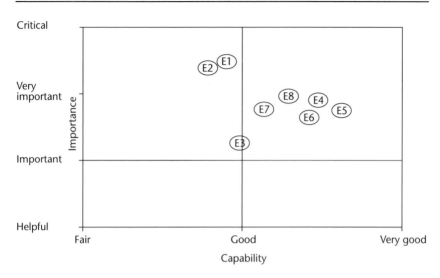

E1 = Ensuring commitment of employees
E2 = Establishing effective communication
E3 = Providing counselling and welfare
E4 = Ensuring compliance with organization policy and legal requirements
E5 = Handling grievances and discipline
E6 = Consultation and negotiation
E7 = Ensuring equality of opportunity
E8 = Health and safety.

The final questions in this questionnaire concerned the work processes through which all HR services are provided to internal clients. This data is provided in Figure 2.7.

Section F – Work Processes

Respondents rated all Work Processes as very important for long-term organization success. Four of the six work processes were also rated as being provided effectively, including:

F1   Assessing client needs and opportunities for service delivery

F2   Designing and selecting the best tools and processes

FIGURE 2.7   Personnel's view of themselves – Work Processes

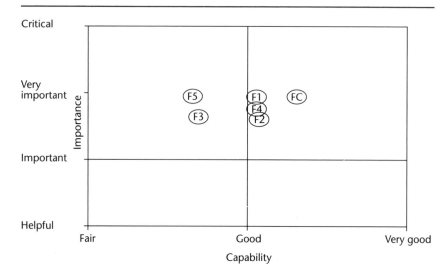

F1 = Assessing clients' needs and opportunities
F2 = Designing and selecting processes
F3 = Marketing and promotion
F4 = Implementation of HR services
F5 = Monitoring and evaluating services
FC = Establishing policy for personnel

F4   Implementing HR services

FC   Establishing HR policies and procedures.

Respondents rated the following two work processes as being delivered less effectively:

F3   Marketing and promoting the service internally

F5   Monitoring and evaluating service effectiveness.

The last point provides the main theme for this book, the assumption being that by improved monitoring and evaluation of HR service effectiveness we will be able to improve our contribution to overall organization effectiveness.

The data reported so far provides a set of priorities for improving the delivery of HR services.

To compare your own self-assessment with the national samples we suggest you use a different colour pen, copy the scattergrams provided earlier and indicate where your ratings are in comparison with the samples. This should enable you to establish the areas of priorities for your organization and compare them with the areas of priority identified by other senior practitioners. By going through this process, you and possibly all the HR practitioners in your organization will be able to crystallize your view on functional strengths and areas for improvement. The next chapter will help you develop a broader perspective on functional competence by collecting feedback from your internal customers.

CHAPTER THREE

Collecting feedback from internal customers

This chapter describes how to collect feedback from the internal clients of the HR department. Data on client perceptions of the importance of various services and of the department's ability to deliver effective service in each area is described in relation to its utility for setting priorities for improvement. Sample findings from 24 case study organizations provide benchmarks for analysing data from your own organization.

Up to this point we have used the self-assessment data provided by HR practitioners such as yourself to identify areas of priorities for service improvement within the department. But there are clear limitations to using self-assessment information as the only guide for action. After all we may be wrong. Therefore, to improve effectiveness we need to be clear about what HR services our internal customers consider are important to the long-term success of the organization and what services they feel are not being provided well.

It is, therefore, ideal that before establishing a clear set of priorities for improvement you should use a process similar to that used for self-assessment to gain information from your internal customers, senior and middle managers. This will enable you to ascertain how they feel about the services that you are and should be providing to them.

Once again the work of the Personnel Standards Lead Body is very significant in this area. As part of the overall project plan 24 leading organizations in the private and public sectors have worked together with the Personnel Standards Lead Body to compare data provided by HR practitioners with data provided by line managers. This data includes ratings about what services are perceived to be important to organization success and where there are fundamental gaps in the quality of service currently being provided.

The organizations included in this project were British Gas, Boots the Chemist, RAC, BBC, Rhone Poulenc, the Defence Research Agency, Parcel Force, a local authority and a number of leading NHS trusts. In general, these organizations are household names and, in our opinion, provide examples of good quality HR service. One can, therefore, assume that the benchmark provided by the data from these organizations may be a relatively stretching target for the average organization.

Figures 3.1 to 3.5 illustrate the services provided by HR functions in these 24 case study organizations. To preserve the confidentiality of the information for each individual organization, we are providing here the aggregate findings for the case study organizations as a whole. These data, in aggregate, represent the opinions of 431 HR practitioners and of 1,076 senior and middle line managers from the case study organizations. The first set of findings, shown in Figure 3.1, relate to ratings of HR services in the area of Strategy and Organization.

A number of issues can be highlighted when comparing these self-assessments of HR practitioners with the feedback from line managers in the same 24 organizations.

First, the overall pattern of the relative positioning of the items as rated by the two types of respondent is very similar. The overall order of items from right to left is consistent (A1, A2, A3, A4, A5). This common order of ratings suggests that both HR practitioners and line managers have a very similar view about the relative importance of services in the area of Strategy and Organization and about the capability of the HR department to deliver effectively in these areas.

Second, the self-assessment data and the line managers' rating are extremely similar judging the importance of these HR services to the long-term success of the organization. The following four services were judged to be very important by both populations:

A1   Contributing to the overall strategy of the organization

A2   Developing personnel strategies and plans

A3   Developing effective organization structures and work processes

A4   Facilitating the organization values and culture as required to support its strategy.

Only A5 (Facilitating external relations) was rated by both sets of respondents as less important.

Finally, the key differences between the self-assessment ratings of HR practitioners and those of line managers are in how they judge the HR function's ability to deliver an effective service. Line managers give lower

FIGURE 3.1   Strategy and Organization:

(a) Line managers' view of Personnel

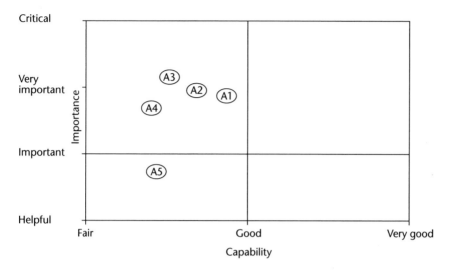

(b) Personnel's view of themselves

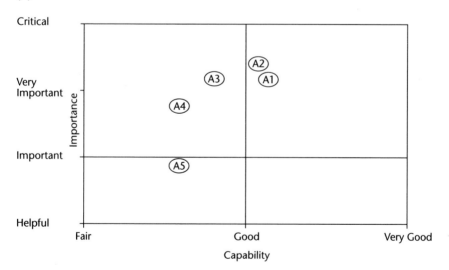

A1 = Organization strategy
A2 = Personnel strategy
A3 = Structure and work processes
A4 = Values and culture
A5 = External relations

ratings, especially when assessing HR's capability to contribute to the development of the business strategy and, surprisingly, even to the development of a personnel strategy.

The next set of findings, shown in Figure 3.2, relate to the area of Resourcing.

A great deal of similarity emerges between the self-assessment ratings of HR practitioners and those of line managers in these organizations when judging services in the area of Resourcing.

Contrary to the findings from the sample of 978 heads of HR (reviewed in Chapter Two), both sets of respondents in these 24 case study organizations rate the following services as being very important to long-term organization success while the current quality of service delivered by the HR function in these areas can be improved:

B1   Establishing resourcing plans

B3   Internal resourcing (deployment) of staff

B4   Identifying individual potential.
And to some degree B5 (Releasing people from the organization).

The use of sub-contractors and temporary staff (B6) is rated by both sets of respondents as an area of service that is less important. This finding is similar to that of the sample in Chapter Two. It is surprising given the increased sub-contracting of non-core services in many organizations.

The main difference between the ratings of the two samples is in relation to external recruitment and selection (B2). Both agree that this service is important to long-term organizational success. But while HR practitioners perceive the current quality of service provided in this area to be high (between 'good' and 'very good') line managers see this as an area where the service should be improved (since their average rating is less than 'good').

The next set of data relates, shown in Figure 3.3, to Development.

The data from the two samples is very similar when rating both importance and capability in this area. This data is also similar to that reported in Chapter Two.

In general, all four services in this area are rated, both by HR practitioners and by the line managers in their organizations, as being very important for long-term organization success.

This finding is very encouraging since it indicated widespread backing for the potential contribution of effective performance planning and review processes, training, long-term individual development and team development processes as vehicles for improving overall organization effectiveness. There is also a shared view about problems in service delivery in this area of

FIGURE 3.2   Resourcing

(a) Line managers' view of Personnel

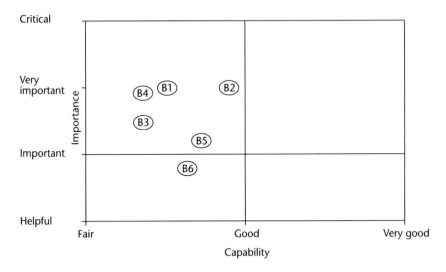

(b) Personnel's view of themselves

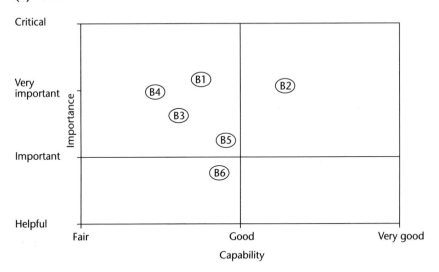

B1 = **Resourcing plans**
B2 = **Recruitment and selection**
B3 = **Internal resourcing**
B4 = **Identifying individual potential**
B5 = **Releasing people**
B6 = **Using sub-contractors and temporary staff.**

FIGURE 3.3   Enhance Individual and Group Performance

(a) Line managers' view of Personnel

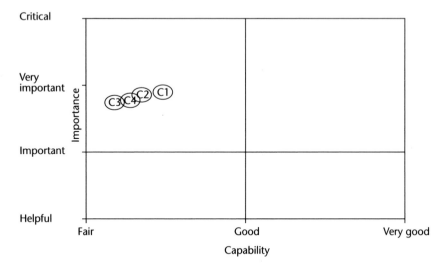

(b) Personnel's view of themselves

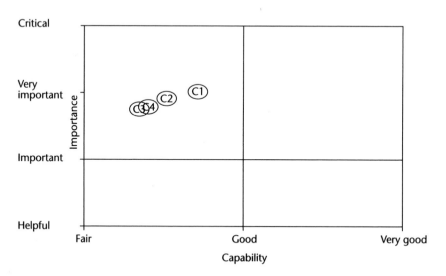

C1= Performance management
C2= Enhancing individual capabilities
C3= Long-term individual development
C4= Team development.

HR management. Both HR practitioners and line managers in these 24 case study organizations agree that a great deal can be improved.

The next set of findings relates to the area of Reward Management (Figure 3.4). The findings from both sets of respondents are very similar when judging services in this area.

Both agree that the following, more administrative services are important to organization success and that they are currently being delivered effectively:

D3   Agreeing terms and conditions of employment

D4   Paying employees

D5   Administering benefits.

Similarly, both the HR practitioners and their line managers agree that the following, more strategic services are very important to long-term organizational success but that the quality of service delivery in these areas should be improved:

D1   Developing a reward strategy

D2   Establishing effective criteria for rewarding employees.

The fifth set of services focuses on Relations with Employees (Figure 3.5). Once again, there was a great deal of consistency between the self-assessment of HR practitioners and line managers' perceptions about the provision of services in these areas.

Both agreed that the following, more traditional industrial relations type services were very important to long-term organizational success and were currently being delivered effectively:

E4   Ensuring compliance with organization policy and legal require-ments

E5   Handling grievance and discipline

E7   Ensuring equal opportunities

E8   Health and safety at work.

Both groups agreed that the following, Organizational Development type services were very important or even critical to long-term organization success but that the quality of service in these areas must be improved:

E1   Ensuring the commitment of employees in times of change

E2   Facilitating effective internal communications

There were small differences in rating the effectiveness of current services provided in the remaining areas where line managers in these organizations thought that service quality was somewhat lower:

E3   Providing counselling and welfare

E6   Consultation and negotiation with individuals and groups.

The final set of findings concerns the work processes used to deliver HR services across the range described here. Both HR practitioners and line managers in the 24 case study organizations were asked to rate the importance of various work processes and functional capability to perform them effectively, regardless of the content of the specific service involved. This data is presented in Figure 3.6.

In general the ratings of the two sets of respondent are relatively similar. Both agree that most of these work processes are important to long-term organization success and that there is room for improvement in every work process involved.

The self-assessment data from HR practitioners suggests that the key areas for improvement are:

F3   Marketing and promoting the service internally

F5   Monitoring and evaluating service effectiveness.

These ratings are consistent with the national sample data reported in Chapter Two.

The findings from line managers in these 24 organizations are very revealing. They also agree that monitoring and evaluating service effectiveness (F5) is very important to long-term organization success. But in contrast to the HR practitioners, line managers in these organizations view the need to market and promote services internally as being less than important. This may suggest a view that the main priority, from the perspective of the function's internal customers, is not in marketing but in service improvement.

Everyone seems to agree that almost the entire range of HR services is very important to long-term organization success. This consistent finding represents good news about the commitment of over a thousand

FIGURE 3.4 Compensation and Benefits

(a) Line managers' view of Personnel

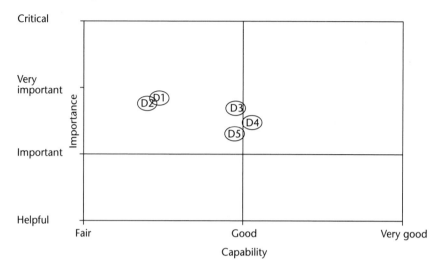

(b) Personnel's view of themselves

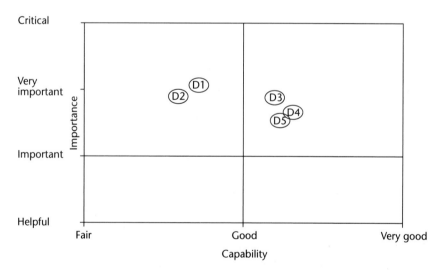

D1= Devising reward strategy
D2= Establishing criteria for reward
D3= Agreeing terms and conditions of employment
D4= Paying employees
D5= Administering benefits.

FIGURE 3.5 Relations with Employees

(a) Line managers' view of Personnel

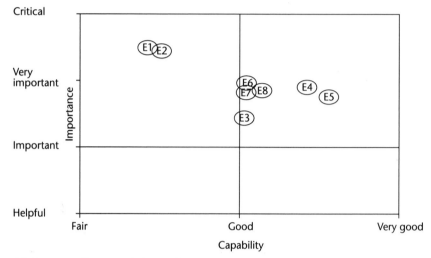

(b) Personnel's view of themselves

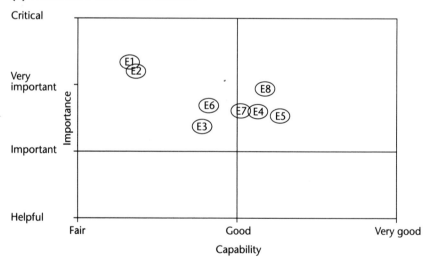

E1 = Ensuring commitment of employees
E2 = Establishing effective communication
E3 = Providing counselling and welfare
E4 = Ensuring compliance with organization policy and legal requirements
E5 = Handling grievances and discipline
E6 = Consultation and negotiation
E7 = Ensuring equality of opportunity
E8 = Health and safety.

FIGURE 3.6 Work Processes

(a) Line managers' view of Personnel

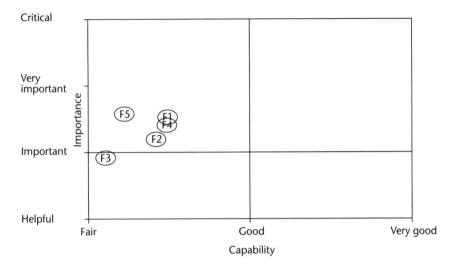

(b) Personnel's view of themselves

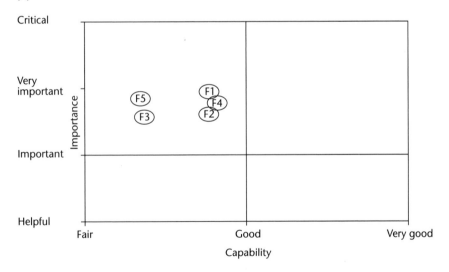

F1 = Assessing clients' needs and opportunities
F2 = Designing and selecting processes
F3 = Marketing and promotion
F4 = Implementation of HR services
F5 = Monitoring and evaluating services.

line managers in these case study organizations to the potential contribution of HR services to business performance.

Our task at the moment seems to be to ensure that we provide this potential contribution more effectively. This emphasis on improving service delivery is especially important in the light of the consistently lower ratings given by line managers than by HR practitioners.

The data from these organizations can serve as a benchmark for your review of the relative importance and quality of HR management services provided in your organization.

You can use the questionnaire in the Appendix to solicit the opinions of all the HR staff in your function. As for line managers, you may want to send the questionnaire to all the senior managers and to a large sample of those middle managers who tend to be your day-to-day customers.

A covering letter explaining your wish to improve service quality as the basis for soliciting their feedback should be sufficient to ensure a high rate of response (we had a return rate of about 65% from line managers and about 90% from HR staff).

Once collected, you can analyse the data by calculating averages and indicating them on the scattergrams provide earlier in this chapter. This data will provide you with an excellent foundation to go back to your line management clients to discuss in more detail what you now understand to be priority areas for improvement and how you intend to deal with them.

CHAPTER FOUR

Budget and activity analysis

This chapter focuses on a review of the HR budget and an analysis of staff activities as a basis for understanding current service priorities. Comparing existing resource allocation to functional priorities will highlight mismatches and identify required changes. An example of the use of these processes in one company is provided for illustration.

Up to now, we have examined the priorities of the HR function from the point of view of those who deliver the service. We have then compared these perceptions with those of our clients, determining what they see as important for the short- and long-term success of the business and where they see major service quality problems. In improving the HR function, however, we also need assessment information to enable us to compare perceived priorities with actual ones. One of the best ways to examine actual priorities is to review current resource allocations. If there is a mismatch between our priorities, those of our clients and those as expressed in resource allocation we should evaluate the situation in more detail and either change our perceptions of what should be done or change the existing pattern of functional activities.

The process of examining resource allocation can be called a budget and activity analysis process. In its simplest form it involves examining the types of activity carried out by the HR function and the amount of people and monetary resources that are allocated to each of them. In effect, it is possible to conduct this type of activity analysis at various levels. At the highest and simplest level, one can take the overall people and monetary budgets and allocate them to gross activity categories. This exercise is extremely useful in gaining high-level understanding of the distribution of resources as an indicator of priorities in comparison with the perceived priorities expressed by ourselves and our customers. This analysis could highlight large-scale mismatches. A more detailed activity analysis can look at the types of work done by individual HR employees and summing this information up to the functional level. This type of analysis is much more useful if one is attempting not only to realign priorities but also to use the exercise as a basis for efficiency improvement. Both types of activity analysis are described below.

Conducting a high-level activity analysis is a relatively straightforward operation; we are attempting to get an overall feel for the priorities used in resource allocation rather than precise figures. The first task is, therefore, to have a clear view of the total resources available to the function. Those would usually come directly from the budget and would involve resources of staff as full-time equivalents at various levels and monetary resources, which include not just staff costs but all other costs associated with the function. In some organizations this relatively simple requirement may be quite complex because a number of types of resources used by the function may not be shown in its budget. For example, space costs may be carried in a facilities budget and not allocated to each individual department. In some organizations training budgets may not be centralized and each business unit could have its own resources for such activities.

Obviously, in order to understand priorities it is important to have a high-level view of all resources used by the function regardless of where the organization's financial accounting procedures classify them. This process of resource identification is much more difficult in a decentralized function, where a large proportion of HR service resources appear in line management budgets. For assessing high-level priorities, however, you should be able to estimate even decentralized resources by multiplying numbers of staff employed by an estimated average cost per head.

Once you have a view of the total resources available, the activity analysis involves dividing those resources according to the types of service provided by the function. The best way to calculate this is to use the classification of the range of HR services arrived at through the functional map developed by the Personnel Standards Lead Body, as described in earlier chapters. A typical form for this process is shown in Figure 4.1.

This form should enable you, in a relatively straightforward fashion, to assess how the total amount of resources available to your HR function is spread across the services you provide. You can then compare the relative importance assigned to a service (by the proportion of resources provided for it) with the relative priority established for that service according to your own and your customers' perceptions. This can be illustrated in graphical form as in the data in Figure 4.2, taken from a real case study organization.

This shows that the major part of staff costs in this organization are

FIGURE 4.1   A form for analysing resources in relation to services

Current human resource activities

Activity	Staff		Other costs	
	No.	Cost	Variable	Fixed
TOTAL				
1. **Strategy and organization**				
1.1 Contribution to organization strategy				
1.2 Organization structure and work processes (changing, improving)				
1.3 Culture and values (defining, changing)				
2. **Resourcing**				
2.1 Recruitment and selection				
2.2 Internal deployment				
2.3 Releasing (redundancy, retirement)				
2.4 Sub-contractors and temporary staff				
3. **Development**				
3.1 Performance management				
3.2 Training				
3.3 Long-term individual development				
3.4 Team development				
4. **Reward**				
4.1 Levels of reward (job evaluation)				
4.2 Paying employees				
4.3 Administering benefits				
5. **Relations with employees**				
5.1 Ensuring employee commitment				
5.2 Internal communication				
5.3 Employee support services (i.e. counselling)				
5.4 Health and Safety				
5.5 Compliance				
5.6 Negotiations with groups and individuals				
5.7 Grievance and discipline				
5.8 Equal opportunities				
6. **Other HR services** (please specify)				
7. **Internal processes**				
7.1 Managing the HR function				
7.2 Internal meetings/co-ordination				
7.3 HR data – input, analysis, presentation				
7.4 Evaluating the effectiveness of HR services				
7.5 Improving existing HR services				
7.6 OTHER INTERNAL PROCESSES (please specify)				

focused on providing Training and Development services (55%). This is
followed by HR services in the areas of Resourcing (20%), and in the area
of Relations with Employees (15%). Reward as well as Strategy and
Organizational services take up only a very small part of HR department
staff costs.

An even more extreme distribution was found when we examined
the allocation of other costs according to the type of HR service provided

FIGURE 4.2   Staff costs by functional area

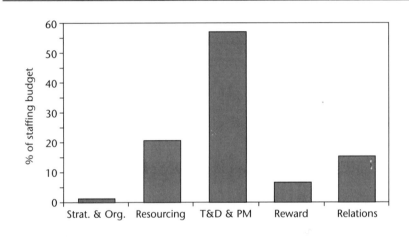

FIGURE 4.3   Other costs by functional area

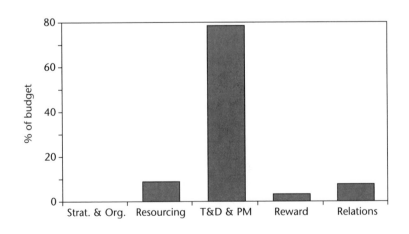

(Figures 4.3 and 4.4). Almost all these resources were focused on Training and Development activities (80%).

In general, therefore, in this organization, most of the HR budget clearly goes to Training and Development services with Resourcing and Relations with Employees trailing at a distance.

This high-level budget analysis becomes much more interesting when we compare the allocation of resources to the expressed priorities. The first comparison is made between the budget and what HR practitioners within this case study organization saw as key business priorities. This data is presented in Figure 4.5.

Staff in this HR function thought that the five service areas were of approximately equal importance to the long-term success of the organization. This perceived importance, however, did not match the allocation of actual staff resources. Training and Development services took up 'too much' of the staff resource, while Strategy and Organizational services and Reward services took up 'too little' staff resource. This pattern of finding does not change significantly when we include other resources in addition to staff costs.

The bar-charts in Figures 4.6 and 4.7 present a similar story by examining internal customer (e.g. line managers') perceptions about the relative importance of different HR activities, as these relate to actual budget allocations.

Once again, the internal customers perceived all areas of the HR service to be of about equal importance to long-term business success.

FIGURE 4.4 Total costs by functional area

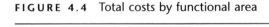

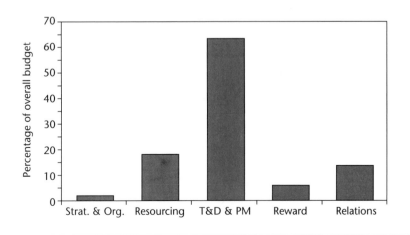

FIGURE 4.5 Personnel's view: importance versus staff allocation

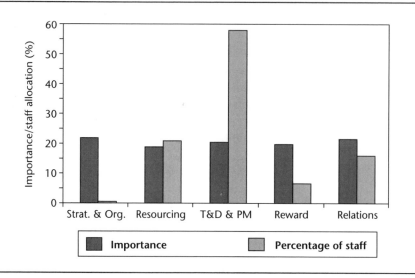

FIGURE 4.6 Personnel's view: importance versus overall budget

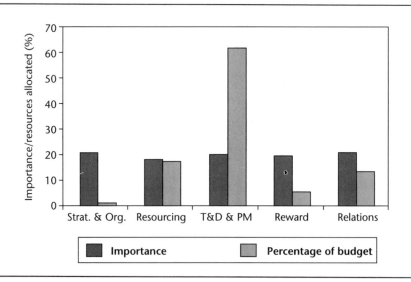

Despite these expressed priorities, however, the actual allocation of the total HR budget indicated a very different set of priorities. The only service area that received a 'correct' share was Resourcing. In contrast, Training and Development services received 'too much' of the resource

FIGURE 4.7 Line management's view: importance versus overall budget

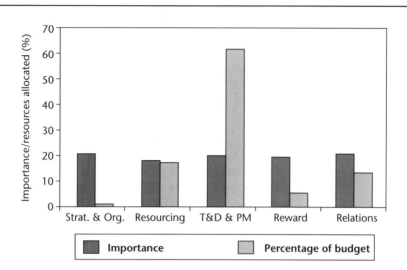

when compared with customer priorities and Strategy and Organizational services received 'too little'. If we assume that the allocation of resources represents, more or less, the real priorities of service delivery, then we can expect clients to be especially unhappy in the areas where resource allocation does not match their expectations.

The next set of findings from this case study organization can be used to examine the relationship between perceived service quality, or functional capability to deliver an effective service in a given area, and the proportion of functional resources that are put into it.

Figure 4.8 shows how line managers' perceptions of the quality of services provided by the HR function relate to budget allocations.

While, in general, these internal customers did not perceive large-scale service quality differences, two areas they assessed as below an acceptable level were Training and Development and Resourcing. Interestingly these were the two areas which received the largest proportion of resources, suggesting that the problem is not one of investment requirements but reflects other types of service quality issues. This finding is fundamental as a basis for service improvement. It indicates that, in this case study organization at least, we do not need to provide more resources to improve services.

Highlighting the gaps between actual resource allocation and perceived customer and professional priorities should enable you to

FIGURE 4.8 Line management view: capability versus total budget

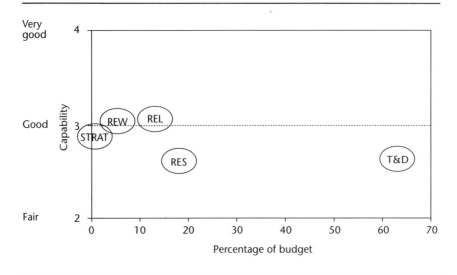

establish the areas in your organization where some decision making is required. Obviously this is not a computer-based decision-making process where one needs to assign actual resources in direct proportion to perceived customer and self-reported importance or to perceived service quality problems (e.g. capability). In some cases there are services that one would judge to be of only medium importance but for which a significant amount of resources are required to provide even a basic level of necessary service. An example would be paying employees. Usually this area is not rated as being the most important for long-term organizational success but, in reality, it does take a certain amount of resources and one cannot imagine a situation where the organization will decide not to provide this service.

In general, however, we would expect the overall allocation of resources to reflect the perception of importance attached to each service area. It is usually helpful, therefore, to take the graphic representation of the gap as illustrated above and use it in discussions within the function and between the function and its key internal customers. This information will help you reach sometimes difficult decisions about services that should and should not be provided given the costs and perceived benefits associated with them.

The relationship between perceived service quality and budget allocation is even more complex. As can be seen from the case study organization data presented earlier, it is possible to spend a very high proportion of functional resources on a given service and still have quality problems. This type of data, however, is very useful for highlighting priority areas for quality improvement, making it possible to create more impact with existing resources. Such data would lead to more in-depth discussions with key internal customers on specifying the criteria for effective service delivery and to find out why they view the current delivery as below the standards required.

Up to this point we have examined activity analysis as a high-level process for establishing the degree of match between perceived importance and actual resource allocation. The same type of technique is also extremely valuable for examining, in much more depth, the nature of activities carried out by individuals within the HR function and the degree to which they can directly add value to functional and organization priorities. The process does not involve managerial assessment of the allocation of resources to activities but rather data collection where all, or a representative sample of, staff members within the function describe how they allocate their time among a set of activities. This individual data is then aggregated up to a total functional level for an overview picture of staff activities. This analysis provides more accurate data when compared with the high-level analysis described earlier. But more important, it enables us to focus on a large proportion of the time, both of a given staff group and across all staff in the HR function, that does not directly add value to the overall effectiveness of the organization.

For a more detailed activity analysis it is important to form a staff task force within the HR function made up of people who understand the variety of services provided. This task force usually starts by creating a list that covers the HR staff's activities. Once again the map of HR services developed by the Personnel Standards Lead Body described earlier can be a very useful guide to developing an initial list of activities. Specific tailoring will be needed to ensure that the list covers most of what staff members are doing at any given time. Typically one would expect around 25 to 40 activities to provide the basis for this analysis. A shorter list of generic activities may also be helpful to cover other time-consuming events. These may include meetings, phone calls, planning etc. In general the overall focus should be to create a finite list of activities enabling most staff to describe about 90% of their daily work.

This list of activities is then used to generate a small number of questionnaires that can be distributed to staff across the function asking them to describe what they are doing. In some cases, staff are asked only to indicate an overall percentage of time in an average month (or week) that they devote to each type of activity. This kind of activity analysis is aimed at providing a higher-level understanding of what staff think they are doing over a general period of time, ignoring differences between one day and another. In some cases, there may be large seasonal variations and it could be helpful to ask staff to provide an analysis of their activities by quarters or some other relevant time frame. As in the high-level analysis described earlier, it is useful to ask people to describe their overall time distribution in percentage terms, thereby ensuring that they describe everything that is being done.

An example of a typical analysis form is provided overleaf.

The summary of data from individual activity analysis forms tends to be relatively straightforward. First of all the data from individuals is aggregated to a sub-functional service level (e.g. training) and then to a total functional level across the data collection period. By this aggregation we can find a number of useful lists of information. From an efficiency point of view, a number of problems will emerge from this data. The first is duplication: large numbers of staff in different sub-functional areas will report doing the same kind of activity. Usually this duplication will provide an opportunity for streamlining so that fewer people and areas are involved in providing a service, thereby requiring less coordination and/or less duplication of effort.

The second type of efficiency improvement to come out of an activity analysis will involve situations of over-involvement. Some areas may find themselves doing a wide array of activities related to the provision of different services. This would reduce the capability of individuals to focus on key output requirements. It is usually helpful for individuals and teams to focus on a relatively small number of tasks with a direct link to a perceived output so that they can be aware of how well they are doing and can focus their efforts towards improvement. In some organizations services are broken down across a large number of sub-sections so that each is engaged in only a small part of providing the overall service and in parallel is involved in other activities related to the provision of other services. This lack of focus makes it very difficult for individuals and teams to improve on service provision and may serve to indicate a need to restructure the function in a more focused way.

The third type of efficiency improvement will emerge in the form of a large proportion of people's time not focused on service delivery. You will find staff involved in generic activities such as planning, meetings, data reporting and filing, none of which adds a direct value to the functional delivery of service or to organizational effectiveness as a whole. This information does not mean that the activity can be cut immediately but it will point to areas where much more in-depth examination can result in very large-scale efficiencies.

Current human resource activities

Please indicate below the percentage of time that YOU spend in an average week on each of the following HR areas of service. You may want to refer to the enclosed definitions to assist you in your ratings. Please make sure that the total percentages of your time add up to 100%. Because of the seasonal nature of some of our activities you can indicate variations according to the different seasons. You can complete only the first column if such variations do not exist in your work.

Activity	Percent time spent in a given week			
	Jan.–Mar.	April–June	July–Sept.	Oct.–Dec.
1. Strategy and organization				
1.1 Contribution to organization strategy				
1.2 Organization structure and work processes (changing, improving)				
1.3 Culture and values (defining, changing)				
2. Resourcing				
2.1 Recruitment and selection				
2.2 Internal deployment				
2.3 Releasing (redundancy, retirement,)				
2.4 Sub-contractors and temporary staff				
3. Development				
3.1 Performance management				
3.2 Training				
3.3 Long-term individual development				
3.4 Team development				
4. Reward				
4.1 Levels of reward (job evaluation)				
4.2 Paying employees				
4.3 Administering benefits				
5. Relations with employees				
5.1 Ensuring employee commitment				
5.2 Internal communication				
5.3 Employee support services (i.e. counselling)				
5.4 Health and Safety				
5.5 Compliance				
5.6 Negotiations with groups and individuals				
5.7 Grievance and discipline				
5.8 Equal opportunities				
6. Other HR Services (please specify)				
7. Internal processes				
7.1 Managing the HR function				
7.2 Internal meetings/co-ordination				
7.3 HR data – input, analysis, presentation				
7.4 Evaluating the effectiveness of HR services				
7.5 Improving existing HR services				
7.6 OTHER INTERNAL PROCESSES (please specify)				
Total	100%	100%	100%	100%

In addition to the three types of efficiency improvements outlined above, the data from this more in depth activity analysis will give you much more accurate information about the distribution of resources within the function and the degree to which it matches the allocation of priorities outlined in the previous chapters. Once again, this analysis can be provided in graphical form, making it possible to identify gaps and to use this information as a basis for realigning activities to be more in line with the overall priorities as viewed by the function and by its internal customers.

One case study organization used bar-code technology to develop a more accurate picture of the activities of HR staff. A sample of representative HR staff in key jobs used electronic pens and a set of bar-codes to indicate when they started and ended a given activity. Following the two weeks of data collection it was possible to review the activities, identify problems and use the data to address them. This method was superior to those described before because it gives data about what people are actually doing, rather than what they think they are when asked to describe a typical week.

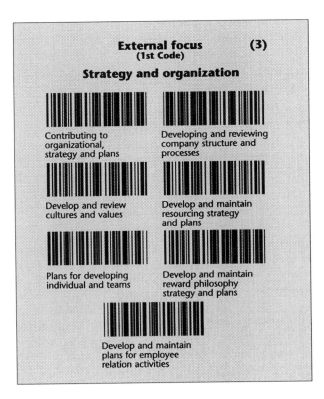

External focus   (3)
(1st Code)
Strategy and organization

Contributing to organizational, strategy and plans

Developing and reviewing company structure and processes

Develop and review cultures and values

Develop and maintain resourcing strategy and plans

Plans for developing individual and teams

Develop and maintain reward philosophy strategy and plans

Develop and maintain plans for employee relation activities

External focus (4)
(1st code)
Resourcing

Recruiting into the
company – candidate
interview

Internal resourcing
– candidate interview

Recruiting into the
company – other

Internal resourcing -
other

Release employee
from company –
candidate interview

Temporary contract
staff through 3rd party

Release employee from
company – other

External focus (5)
(1st code)
Managing development

Establish the performance
planning and review
process

Promote training –
delivery

Promote training –
other

Promote long term
individual development
– delivery

Promote team
development – delivery

Promote long term
individual development
– other

Promote team
development – other

External focus **(6)**
(1st code)
Reward management

Establish levels of
reward for roles
and people

Pay employee –
administration

Manage benefits/
expenses – admin

Pay employee –
other

Manage benefits/
expenses – other

Method **(10)**
(2nd code)

Meeting – personnel

Telephone

Meeting – line management

Meeting – other

Writing

Reading

Inputting data

Data analysis

Personnel needs/lunch break

LOG OFF

CHAPTER 5

Improving the competence of Human Resource staff

This chapter provides an approach for reviewing staff competence to deliver effectively across the range of HR services. By comparing existing staff competence with HR service priorities it is possible to pinpoint training and development as well as resourcing requirements. The chapter also includes sample data from a case study organization to show how to use the process effectively.

So far, we have examined the priorities for the delivery of HR services from an organizational perspective. As service providers, what do we feel are the opinions of our internal customers and how do these compare with our current resource allocations? These are key questions, which enable us to examine what we do well and less well as a staff function.

But our ability to deliver effective service depends not only on where we focus our resources, but also on the individual competence of the HR staff. If they do not have the required competence in the key service areas required by our customers, they will not be able to provide effective service as individuals and we will not be able to perform well as a function.

In evaluating staff competence it is important to use the framework used previously to assess the effectiveness of the function as a whole. This common framework will enable us to compare results both on an individual and organizational level and thereby identify gaps that prevent us from delivering effectively as a functional team. A questionnaire similar to that in Chapters One and Two was developed but this time data was collected with a focus on individuals' capability. All the non-administrative staff in an organization were asked to get together with their boss and complete a questionnaire about their own competence and training requirements across the range of HR services. A sample questionnaire is provided overleaf and in the Appendix.

PERSONNEL STANDARDS LEAD BODY

COMPSCAN

Competence in Personnel: self-assessment

This questionnaire is designed for you and your manager to describe **your** competence in being able to perform a range of Personnel functions.

It will also enable you to specify where you would like to develop further your competence in this field.

This information will be used to identify priority areas for training and development activities in order to improve the quality of our services to the organization.

Name: _____   Job title: _____

Date: _____

Age: _____   Sex: M _____   F _____   Years of Personnel experience: _____

Role: Managerial _____   Professional _____   Administrative _____

I would describe myself as a Personnel: Generalist _____   Specialist _____

Competency in the key functions of Personnel

Listed below are Personnel functions grouped under five headings. We would like you to rate against each function:

- **Importance for current job**
  Please circle the number in the column that best reflects the importance of that function to your success in your current job. Circle zero if the function is not relevant.
- **Current level of competence**
  Please circle the number in the column that best reflects your level of competence in performing each function. We assume that due to previous experience, you will be competent also in functions that do not form part of your current job responsibilities.
- **Training and development needs**
  Please tick (√) this column if you feel that you would benefit from participating in training and development activities to increase your competence in a given function. Please indicate the specific nature of your requirement in the open-ended section provided after each group of functions.

A. Strategy and organization	Importance for current job 1 Not relevant 2 Small part of 3 Important part of 4 Very important for success 5 Critical for success					Current level of competence 1 Not competent 2 Can do only a little in this area 3 Can do most basic things 4 Can do everything well 5 Am a recognized authority					Training and development need
Contribute to the overall **strategy of the organiz-ation** by providing generalist and specialist information and advice	1	2	3	4	5	1	2	3	4	5	☐
Develop and maintain an appropriate **personnel strategy** to support the overall strategy of the organization	1	2	3	4	5	1	2	3	4	5	☐
Enable the creation of an **organization structure and work processes** that maximize the performance of people at work	1	2	3	4	5	1	2	3	4	5	☐
Facilitate the development of **organization values and culture** required to support its strategy	1	2	3	4	5	1	2	3	4	5	☐

Specific training and development needs: _____

_____

_____

B. Resourcing											
Develop and maintain **workforce planning** to support current and future requirements	1	2	3	4	5	1	2	3	4	5	☐
Recruit and select people into the organization	1	2	3	4	5	1	2	3	4	5	☐
Optimize the **deployment of staff** within the organization	1	2	3	4	5	1	2	3	4	5	☐
Identify **individual potential** to develop and meet future resourcing requirements	1	2	3	4	5	1	2	3	4	5	☐
Release people from the organization (e.g. retirement, redundancy)	1	2	3	4	5	1	2	3	4	5	☐
Engage non-core and temporary staff	1	2	3	4	5	1	2	3	4	5	☐

Specific training and development needs: _____

_____

_____

C. Development	Importance for current job 1 Not relevant 2 Small part of 3 Important part of 4 Very important for success 5 Critical for success					Current level of competence 1 Not competent 2 Can do only a little in this area 3 Can do most basic things 4 Can do everything well 5 Am a recognized authority					Training and development need
Establish and maintain **performance management** processes	1	2	3	4	5	1	2	3	4	5	☐
Establish **training opportunities** to enhance individual competence	1	2	3	4	5	1	2	3	4	5	☐
Promote **longer-term individual development** processes	1	2	3	4	5	1	2	3	4	5	☐
Facilitate **team development** processes	1	2	3	4	5	1	2	3	4	5	☐

Specific training and development needs:_____

_____

_____

D. Reward management											
Develop and maintain a **reward strategy** (e.g. pay, benefits)	1	2	3	4	5	1	2	3	4	5	☐
Establish and maintain the criteria for ensuring appropriate **level of reward** (e.g. job evaluation)	1	2	3	4	5	1	2	3	4	5	☐
Implement and maintain processes to define employees **terms and conditions** of employment	1	2	3	4	5	1	2	3	4	5	☐
Pay contracted employees and others	1	2	3	4	5	1	2	3	4	5	☐
Administer **benefits** and other payments	1	2	3	4	5	1	2	3	4	5	☐

Specific training and development needs:_____

_____

_____

E. Relations with employees	Importance for current job 1 Not relevant 2 Small part of 3 Important part of 4 Very important for success 5 Critical for success					Current level of competence 1 Not competent 2 Can do only a little in this area 3 Can do most basic things 4 Can do everything well 5 Am a recognized authority					Training and development need
Develop and maintain **commitment of employees** in times of change (e.g. support change programmes)	1	2	3	4	5	1	2	3	4	5	☐
Promote effective **communication** within the organization	1	2	3	4	5	1	2	3	4	5	☐
Provide **counselling and welfare** support for the mutual benefit of the organization and the individual	1	2	3	4	5	1	2	3	4	5	☐
Ensure **compliance** with Personnel-related legislation and internal policies	1	2	3	4	5	1	2	3	4	5	☐
Provide processes for handling **grievances and discipline**	1	2	3	4	5	1	2	3	4	5	☐
Consult and/or **negotiate** with employees and/or their representatives to facilitate achievement of organizational goals	1	2	3	4	5	1	2	3	4	5	☐
Promote and ensure **equality of opportunity**	1	2	3	4	5	1	2	3	4	5	☐
Establish and maintain processes for ensuring **health and safety** at work	1	2	3	4	5	1	2	3	4	5	☐

Specific training and development needs: _____
_____
_____

F. Work processes in service delivery

So far we have presented Personnel functions and asked you to indicate their importance for your success in your job and also your level of competence in performing them.

In addition we would like your assessment about importance and your level of competence in performing the following work processes across a range of Personnel functions.

Work processes in service delivery	Importance for current job 1 Not relevant 2 Small part of 3 Important part of 4 Very important for success 5 Critical for success					Current level of competence 1 Not competent 2 Can do only a little in this area 3 Can do most basic things 4 Can do everything well 5 Am a recognized authority					Training and development need
Assess **needs and opportunities** to provide and improve Personnel services	1	2	3	4	5	1	2	3	4	5	☐
Design and select **techniques and processes** for providing Personnel services	1	2	3	4	5	1	2	3	4	5	☐
Market and promote the advantage of utilizing Personnel services	1	2	3	4	5	1	2	3	4	5	☐
Implement and enable others to implement Personnel services											
at a **managerial** level	1	2	3	4	5	1	2	3	4	5	☐
at a **professional** level	1	2	3	4	5	1	2	3	4	5	☐
at an **administrative** level	1	2	3	4	5	1	2	3	4	5	☐
Monitor and evaluate the effectiveness of Personnel services	1	2	3	4	5	1	2	3	4	5	☐

Specific training and development needs:_____
_____
_____

G. General utilization

In general, to what degree do you feel that your current job makes it possible for you to perform to the best of your capability?

☐ 0 – Not at all ☐ 1 – To a small extent ☐ 2 – Mostly ☐ 3 – To a large degree ☐ 4 – Completely

Comments: _____
_____
_____

The sample data provided in Figure 5.1 illustrates the use of this questionnaire in one case study organization. Seventy-one non-administrative staff in the HR function got together with their managers and completed the questionnaire. Data was analysed to establish the key areas that staff consider important for their job but where they, and their managers, rate competence to be less than what is required.

This data shows that while 76% of the staff rated competencies in the area of Strategy and Organization as important for their job, less than half of them were rated as competent in delivering service in this area. Put another way, 31 out of 54 staff members did not have the required level of competence.

In earlier chapters we saw that HR management services in Strategy and Organization are perceived by line managers to be very important to the long-term success of their organizations. Moreover, we saw that the current capability of the HR function to deliver effective service in these areas was rated as low. The data presented here about the competence of individual practitioners shows that many of them whose job requires competence in these areas do not possess the required capability. This individual skill gap is probably one of the major reasons why, as a function, we cannot deliver an appropriate level of service.

The data in Figure 5.2 shows the training requirements considered to be relevant for staff within the competency areas of Strategy and

FIGURE 5.1   Section A: Strategy and Organization

| | | **Competence** | | |
		Low	High	Total
Importance	High	**31** 44% (Training and development need)	**23** 32% (Well-placed)	**54** 76%
	Low	**17** 24% (Well-placed)	—	**17** 24%
	Total	**48** 68%	**23** 32%	**71**

FIGURE 5.2 Training and development needs: Strategy and Organization

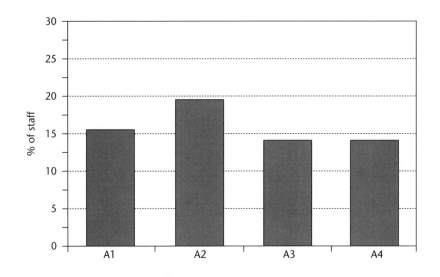

A1 = **Contribute to the overall strategy of the organization by providing generalist and specialist information and advice**
A2 = **Develop and maintain an appropriate Personnel strategy to support the overall strategy of the organization**
A3 = **Enable the creation of an organization structure and work processes that maximize the performance of people at work**
A4 = **Facilitate the development of organization values and culture required to support its strategy.**

Organization. The percentage bars represent the number of HR staff who need additional training in each area of activity.

This data shows that a significant number of HR staff in this organization require training in the areas of Strategy and Organization. The most important area for training was that concerned with developing and maintaining an appropriate HR strategy to support the overall strategy of the organization. Nineteen percent of the HR staff in this organization agreed with their managers that they need training in this area. But in the other service areas, a significant number of HR staff were also rated as requiring additional training.

Another example relates to staff competence in Resourcing. The relevant data is presented in Figure 5.3 as the percentage of HR staff who, in discussions between themselves and their managers, identified areas where they require additional training.

FIGURE 5.3   Section B: Resourcing

		Competence		
		Low	High	Total
Importance	High	**23** 32% (Training and development need)	**33** 47% (Well-placed)	**56** 79%
	Low	**13** 18% (Well-placed)	**2** 3% (Misplaced)	**15** 21%
	Total	**36** 50%	**35** 50%	**71**

Figure 5.3 shows that in this case study organization 79% of the HR staff rated competencies in the area of Resourcing as important to their job. Of those who rated it as important, however, 40% or so were considered not to possess the required level of competence for providing Resourcing services effectively (23 out of 56 staff members).

To better understand the nature of staff competence requirements in this area we can examine which specific service capabilities have been highlighted as requirements for HR staff training. This data is presented in Figure 5.4 where the percentage score indicated by each bar represents the number of staff for whom a given topic was raised by themselves and their manager as a training requirement.

Training needs were indicated as relevant for some staff in all areas of Resourcing but the widest applicability was in the development of workforce planning to support current and future business requirements (17% of staff) and in identifying individual potential to develop and meet future resourcing requirements (where over 20% of staff and their managers indicated a need for training in this area).

It is relevant to compare these findings with those in earlier chapters on line management feedback about Resourcing services. Line managers indicated that Resourcing services were very important to the long-term success of the organization. Regarding capability, however, the picture was somewhat more complex. Line managers indicated that the HR function in their organization was providing an acceptable level of service

FIGURE 5.4   Training and development needs: Resourcing

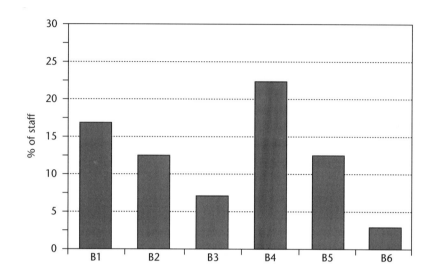

B1 = Develop and maintain workforce planning to support current and
      future requirements
B2 = Recruit people into the organization
B3 = Optimize the deployment of staff within the organization
B4 = Identify individual potential to develop and meet future resourcing
      requirements
B5 = Release people from the organization (eg. retirement, redundancy)
B6 = Engage non-core and temporary staff.

when dealing with external recruitment and selection. But resource planning and the identifying of individuals with long-term potential were considered areas where the HR function was not performing effectively.

The data provided here about the capabilities of individual staff members sheds some light on this pattern of service delivery. In discussion with their managers, a significant number of HR staff identified resource planning and the ability to recognize high-potential individuals as areas where they should receive additional training. One can assume that by improving competence in these areas the HR function will be able to deliver an effective Resourcing service.

The third set of competencies relate to Development. Data on managers and staff rating is presented in Figure 5.5.

The data in this figure shows that 89% of HR staff and their

FIGURE 5.5   Section C: Development

		Competence		Total
		Low	High	
	High	**27** 39% (Training and development need)	**35** 50% (Well-placed)	**62** 89%
Importance	Low	**6** 8% (Well-placed)	**2** 3% (Misplaced)	**8** 11%
	Total	**33** 47%	**37** 53%	**70**

managers in this organization rated competencies in Development as important for performing effectively in their current job. When rating competence, however, about 40% for whom this area was considered to be important were rated as lacking the required level of competence (27 out of 62 HR staff members). The specific training requirements rated as relevant for staff in this area of Development are indicated in Figure 5.6 by the percentage of staff for whom each topic was considered to be relevant.

Almost all the competencies in this area of Development were considered to be relevant for a large proportion of the HR staff. Specifically, many staff and their managers indicated the need for training in how to establish and maintain performance management processes (23%), how to promote longer-term individual development processes (22%) and how to facilitate team development processes (28%).

Once again it is very interesting to compare this data about the capability of individual staff members with the line managers' ratings of the HR function as a whole. In general line managers considered the area of Development to be very important to the long-term success of the organization. The HR function, however, was considered to be not very effective in delivering any of the services in this area. These ratings by line managers correspond to the ratings of staff competence by themselves in discussion with their managers. A very large number of HR staff were

FIGURE 5.6 Training and development needs: Improving individual and group performance

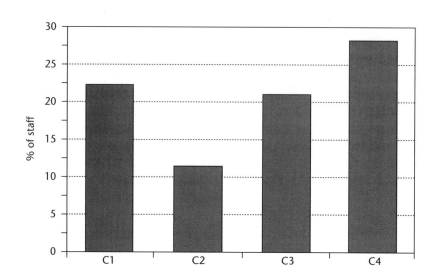

C1 = **Establish and maintain performance management processes**
C2 = **Establish training opportunities to enhance individual competence**
C3 = **Promote longer-term individual development processes**
C4 = **Facilitate team development processes.**

FIGURE 5.7 Section D: Reward Management

		Competence		
		Low	High	Total
Importance	High	**13** 20% (Training and development need)	**11** 17% (Well-placed)	**24** 37%
	Low	**41** 62% (Well-placed)	**1** 1% (Misplaced)	**42** 63%
	Total	**54** 82%	**12** 18%	**66**

perceived to be less than competent in these areas and training requirements were indicated as being very relevant for many.

The fourth area of competence focused on Reward Management. The relevant data from the case study organization is presented in Figure 5.7.

This figure demonstrates the fact that Reward Management is a more specialized competence area within the HR function. Only 37% of staff and their managers rated competencies in this area as important to their current job. Despite the specialized nature of job requirements in this area, a problem is revealed in the ratings for staff competence. Of those who, together with their managers, indicated that Reward Management was an important part of their job, more than 50% were rated as less than competent in performing the required tasks in this area (13 out of 24 staff members).

The information about staff training requirements enables us to understand this problem in somewhat more detail. The distribution of training needs in reward management is indicated in Figure 5.8 as the

FIGURE 5.8   Training and development needs: Compensation and Benefits

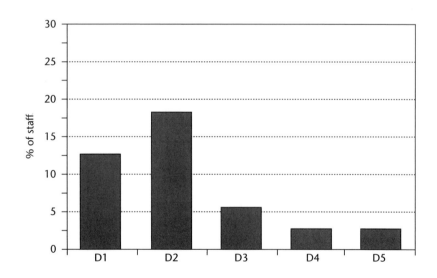

D1 = Develop and maintain a reward strategy (e.g. pay, benefits)
D2 = Establish and maintain the criteria for ensuring appropriate level of reward (e.g. job evaluation)
D3 = Implement and maintain processes to define employees' terms and conditions of employment
D4 = Pay contracted employees and others
D5 = Administer benefits and other payments.

percentage of staff who, together with their managers, indicated a need for training in each area.

The key competencies in which training needs have been identified for a significant number of staff were related to developing and maintaining a reward strategy (13%) and to establishing and maintaining the criteria for ensuring appropriate levels of reward (16%). These findings are also very similar to the organizational data reported in the previous chapters. Both HR staff and line managers in the larger sample of 24 case study organizations presented earlier indicated the importance of the first two Reward Management competencies and the need to improve service in these areas. The wider organizational need is now matched, in the data from this case study, with the need for improving the competence of individual staff as a foundation for improving overall functional competence.

The fifth set of case study data relates to competencies in the area of Relations with Employees. These included competencies both in the area of organizational development (i.e. staff commitment) and competencies in the more traditional areas of employee relations (i.e. negotiation with individuals and groups). The relevant data is given in Figure 5.9.

In general 86% of staff rated competencies in the area of Relations with Employees as important for their current job. On the other hand, when considering only those staff who need to be competent in this area,

FIGURE 5.9   Section E: Relations with Employees

		Competence		
		Low	High	Total
Importance	High	**27** 38% (Training and development need)	**34** 48% (Well-placed)	**61** 86%
	Low	**9** 13% (Well-placed)	**1** 1% (Misplaced)	**10** 14%
	Total	**36** 51%	**35** 49%	**71**

a full 45%, and their managers, indicated that they are not fully competent to provide services in this area (27 out of 61 HR staff).

It is difficult to understand the specific areas where competence improvement is required without looking at staff and managers' assessments of training needs. The nature of the training need identified for HR staff in this case study organization is identified in Figure 5.10.

The main area for staff training in this case study relates to developing and maintaining commitment of employees in times of change (e.g. support organizational change projects) where around 23% of staff and their managers indicated a need for competence development.

FIGURE 5.10 Training and development needs: Relations with Employees

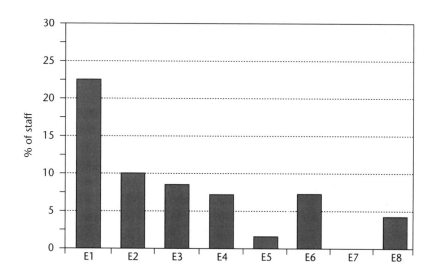

E1 = Develop and maintain commitment of employees in times of change (e.g. support change projects)
E2 = Promote effective communication within the organization
E3 = Provide counselling and welfare support for the mutual benefit of the organization and the individual
E4 = Ensure compliance with Personnel-related legislation and internal policies
E5 = Provide processes for handling grievances and discipline
E6 = Consult and/or negotiate with employees and/or their representatives to facilitate achievement of organizational goals
E7 = Promote and ensure equality of opportunity
E8 = Establish and maintain processes for ensuring health and safety at work.

From the data reported in earlier chapters we saw that this area was also rated as very high priority by line managers in the 24 case studies when they were asked to provide feedback about the performance of the HR function as a whole. The importance attributed to this area highlights the high level of need among HR staff for training so that they can provide effective service to support organizational change.

The final set of data relates to the work processes involved in delivering HR services across the range of content areas. By collecting this type of information it became possible to identify staff competence requirements in the processes that underpin the delivery of effective service independent of the content of the service being delivered. The relevant information is presented in Figure 5.11.

In general 85% of staff in this case study thought that the range of work processes identified here were important for their job performance. Of those who indicated that the process are important, however, only about 50% were rated by themselves and their managers as competent across the range of work processes considered neccessary for effective performance. As with the previous data, it is possible to understand staff requirements better by reviewing the nature of their training needs. The specific training requirements related to these work processes are identified in figure 5.12.

The main areas for competence development were identified as

FIGURE 5.11   Section F: Work Processes in Service Delivery

		Competence		
		Low	High	Total
Importance	High	**30** 43% (Training and development need)	**29** 42% (Well-placed)	**59** 85%
	Low	**10** 15% (Well-placed)	— — (Misplaced)	**10** 15%
	Total	**40** 58%	**29** 42%	**69**

FIGURE 5.12 Training and development needs: Work Processes in Service Delivery

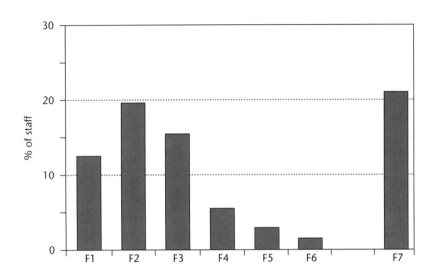

F1 = **Assess needs and opportunities to provide and improve Personnel services**
F2 = **Design and select techniques and processes for providing Personnel services**
F3 = **Market and promote Personnel services**
F4 = **Implement and enable others to implement Personnel services at a managerial level**
F5 = **Implement and enable others to implement Personnel services at a professional level**
F6 = **Implement and enable others to implement Personnel services at an administrative level**
F7 = **Monitor and evaluate the effectiveness of Personnel services.**

assessing internal client needs (13% of staff), designing and selecting the most effective techniques and processes for providing services (19% of staff), marketing and promoting the service internally (16%), and most of all, monitoring and evaluating service effectiveness (22%). The importance of monitoring and evaluating service delivery has also been raised by line managers in their feedback about the HR function as a whole.

In general we see that improving the competence of HR practitioners is not only about providing them with content expertise, but, more significantly, to enable staff to carry out the key processes involved in assessing internal client needs, setting service objectives, developing the best tools and processes, marketing the service internally, implementing it and evaluating service effectiveness as a basis for improvements.

In addition to the data on staff competence in each area of HR service we also used the questionnaire to solicit data about perceived staff use. It was assumed that current levels of competence would, to some degree, influence staff and managers' perceptions of how well they are being utilized in their current job. The relevant data are presented in Figure 5.13.

In general around half the HR staff involved in this process indicated that they were less than fully utilized, since categories 3 and 4 were used by only 43% of staff. It is more significant to note that 14% of staff indicated a No. 2 rating, which says that they are utilized only 'to a small degree' in their current job. These figures are much more disturbing when considered in the context of the rating process itself. The data was derived from ratings completed by individual HR staff, together with their managers. One can assume that we would have had much more disturbing results if the ratings were done confidentially by staff without their managers' knowledge or by a more objective assessment process.

FIGURE 5.13 General utlization of staff

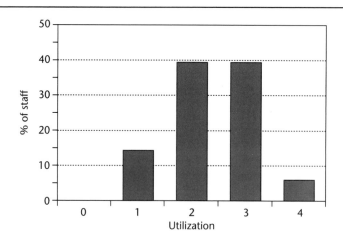

0 Not at all
1 To a small extent
2 Mostly
3 To a large degree
4 Completely

We can assume that, by increasing competence in the designated areas rated by staff and their managers as important for their job, we will be able to increase perceived staff utilization and thereby improve functional performance.

The data reported in this chapter focuses on the assessment of staff competence to provide a range of HR services. This information provides us with the foundation to manage our own people within the function. By ensuring staff competence we also ensure functional capability to deliver. In fact, as we saw through the comparison of this data with the findings from the 24 case studies reported in earlier chapters, the high priority areas for functional improvement as indicated by line managers are, in general, also areas where we do not have competent staff to deliver the service (at least not in the organization for which data has been reported here).

Improving the competence of staff available for delivering HR services may be promoted through training courses or, in many cases, through changing the composition of the current group of staff in the department by looking externally and recruiting those who are already competent in the priority areas. This will not be a short-term process, but it is essential if we want to have the functional capability to deliver high-priority HR services as defined by business requirements.

CHAPTER SIX

Establishing a long-term Human Resource strategy to support the business strategy

This chapter identifies the need to establish a HR strategy to review existing activities and for planning those activities required for supporting the long-term strategy of the organization. The chapter provides a number of aids for relating the HR strategies and activities to the relevant organizational strategies that they support.

We have so far collected a wide array of information about the quality of HR services provided to the organization. This included self-assessment by the practitioners themselves and feedback from internal customers about the range of services provided. An activity analysis was described as well, reviewing where the staff and monetary resources in the function are being spent in comparison to a set of priorities. Finally, a method for reviewing the range of individual capabilities within the function was described, together with the implications about the function's capability to provide some services or its limitations to provide others. All this information can be integrated to ensure that the resources available are geared to the range of services that customers see as important for the future success of the organization. But establishing long-term organizational success is a more complex process.

The feedback from internal customers, which is usually provided from a sample of line managers, is an indication of the quality of HR services provided within the current frame of reference in the organization. Line managers have their own understanding of what they are trying to do at the moment and they have expectations of what we, as a support service, can assist them in achieving. But in order to achieve long-term success, the organization's strategies will sometimes involve radical change. In those circumstances HR practitioners' contributions could and should go beyond the provision of high-quality services to current client expectations. Long-term success may, in many cases, require things that our current clients are not aware of and may in fact result in situations where we cannot provide what line managers require in the short term due to long-term requirements. When the business is expecting to be transformed there will be real questions about how the HR function can support that transformation in a manner that goes beyond short-term line management/customer satisfaction.

It is, therefore, important to go beyond the data collected so far by becoming much clearer about the organization's medium- and long-term strategy. This will enable us to establish the potential contributions that we as a HR function can provide in order to support the achievement of long-term organizational strategic goals.

The first step in establishing this strategic link is to understand the key business strategies that are expected to enable the organization to achieve the mission it set for itself. This is not a simple task. You will usually find in any organization a wide array of strategic documents, which provide a variety of relevant information. The key to under-standing our potential contribution to the long-term strategy is to be able to crystallize the key strategic elements, which can, in turn, provide us with the basis for developing our own strategy. The best place to start is usually the planning department, where you may find documents with some type of business strategy heading. Those documents would tend to focus on an analysis of the environment and a better understanding of potential competitive advantage. What we are looking for, however, is a clear statement of the long-term vision or mission for the organization. What, in relatively specific terms, is this organization trying to achieve in the long term? Once we find a definition of that, which, we hope, is not just a series of platitudes or a verbal description of the current situation, we can try to search for the three, four or maybe five key strategic approaches that the planners assume would lead this organization to achieve its long-term vision. In a number of organizations you will not find a clear definition of high-level strategies for achieving this long-term vision, but many objectives for a variety of sub-functions, although not necessarily an integrated concept. Where there is an integrated concept strategies tend to focus more on defining outputs such as 'we will become more profitable' or 'we will increase our share price' rather than on identifying what we are going to do to achieve them. To support our search for a clear definition of strategy it is also useful to look at annual planning documents. These would usually be associated with the organization's budgetary cycle and would therefore be found in the Finance function. Usually the annual budget requests will begin with a document that outlines the three or four key objectives for the organization and then the resource allocations should in some way be related to these. By combining the more long-term strategy documents with the annual budget documents and maybe one or two planning documents for the key functions, we will have a wide array of definitions of what the organization as a whole sees as key strategic initiatives. In general, we are trying to crystallize a brief definition of the basic approaches that will enable the organization to achieve its long-term vision. Two of the typical items in this category will be 'cost reduction', which tends to be a strategy for most organizations, and 'expansion into new markets' which, in many cases, characterizes organizations' attempts to increase revenues. But other kinds of strategies could focus on product development, on moving to a different type of business and on changing the nature of the process by which the business provides its services to its customers, etc.

Once we have identified the long-term vision and the three, four or five high-level strategies that are expected to deliver it, we should be able to define an HR strategy that can realistically support the achievement of the overall organizational strategies. It is important here to think strategically, beyond the provision of an individual service, because, as we saw before, we can very easily get to a range of 20 to 25 possible HR services. We need to identify three or four guiding principles in setting priorities for each HR service provision. The best process, therefore, is first to try to take each organizational strategy and break it down into what we feel our potential contribution can be. For example, if we take 'cost cutting' as a strategy then clearly reducing manpower costs could well be something that we play a key role in. If we are talking about changing the process by which services are provided then we may have the key contribution in providing the change in the people's capabilities to deliver the new process.

By going through each of the three to five high-level organizational strategies and identifying two or three key contributions that HR professionals can provide to that strategy, we will begin to get a list of potential contributions. This list, however, is too optimistic because it assumes that we address each part of the future planning independently of the other parts. But usually the success of any effort is through integration, where success depends on concentrating energy onto a relatively focused area. Therefore, once we have identified up to 10 or 15 small contributions to the overall success of the organization, it is important to gather all these and compare them to the priorities that we have already collected from the previous efforts described in this book. We will have priorities based on our self-assessment as HR practitioners. We will also have data from line managers as our internal customers about what they see as important and where they see problems in current service delivery. Also, the activity analysis and the assessment of individual capabilities has provided us with some understanding of where effort is being put and where our people's strengths lie. Combining these with the direct contributions that we can add to the organization's strategy should give us a list of maybe 15 to 20 potential high-level strategic contributions that the HR function can make towards the success of the organization. By way of ranking, first as individuals and then combined ranking as a professional team, we can begin to establish a much smaller set of priorities that will enable us to examine our own contribution.

We are aiming to get three, four or five high-level HR strategies to guide all our efforts. This does not mean that as a function we do not provide a wide array of services as described earlier, or that each of those services will not have specific measures and targets of quality, effectiveness and efficiency. But what we need as a function, in a similar way to what the organization needs, is a relatively small set of guiding strategies that will enable us to assign priorities. This would mean that in providing any HR service we will have to watch out for the degree to which that specific service directly contributes to the achievement of these HR strategies and through it, to the achievement of the long-term organization strategy. We are attempting in this way to plan for leverage, where concentration of resources will lead to maximum organizational impact. Typical HR strategies within this type of framework will involve reducing the overall people costs in the organization, improving the performance of individuals, and increasing people flexibility. Any one of these strategic principles will then have specific implications when we examine the targets for any one of the HR services that we provide.

Once we crystallize from the wide array of potential priorities three, four or five high-level HR strategies, we can move to a more specific delineation of the relationship between these strategies and the overall strategies of the organization. The best way to do this is by using a strategy contribution matrix as illustrated in Figure 6.1

This example is from an organization (in the financial sector) with three key strategies. Its long-term success is assumed to be achieved through reducing the current cost base of its operation, through improved relations with its agents in a manner that will encourage them to sell its products rather than those offered by the competition, and through cross selling a wider range of products to its existing customer base. By analysing each of these business strategies this organization came up with a limited range of high-level HR strategies required to support the corporate effort. Cost reduction from a HR point of view is expected to derive from a combined effort at delayering and empowerment.

FIGURE 6.1   Human Resource strategy contribution matrix

Organization Strategy

		Reduce costs	Create close agent relations	Cross sell products	Total
Human Resource Strategy	Delayer and empower	70%	10%	20%	100%
	Create multi-skilling	10%	10%	80%	100%
	Develop performance-oriented culture		50%	50%	100%

This should reduce significantly the size of a very expensive management population and thereby, in the medium term, reduce the payroll.

It is also assumed in the model outlined in Figure 6.1, that some cost reduction will be achieved through multi-skilling, since by creating a more flexible labour force the organization should be able to perform a wider variety of tasks with less manpower. Moreover, multi-skilling is expected to be based on improved labour relations and, therefore, a less rigid allocation of tasks will also contribute to cost reduction.

The second organizational strategy focuses on improving relations with its agents, since a large proportion of its business is conducted through these third parties who sell its products, together with those of its competitors, to the end clients. According to the strategic analysis described here, HR also has a significant role to play in the improvement of relations with these agents.

The main contribution (50%) is expected to come from creating a more performance-oriented culture. By targeting individuals and teams relevant to the improvement of agent relations and by rewarding key behaviours that support the improvement of such relationships, this organization believes that it can do this.

The two other HR strategies are also expected to improve relations with its agents, albeit to a much smaller degree. There is an expectation that delayering and empowerment will create a much leaner organization that is closer to its customers and can therefore deal more effectively with their needs. It is also assumed that empowering those who have day-to-day dealings with agents will enable them to handle urgent requirements in a significantly improved manner without always having to delay decisions by going up the line. This, in their opinion, will create more satisfied agents who will prefer to sell this organization's products. Finally, multi-skilling is also assumed to improve agent relations because a single person will be able to handle a very wide range of agent requirements. This should also create a better contact with each agent and facilitate decision making and therefore agent satisfaction.

The third organization strategy focused on cross selling a wide range of products to its existing direct client base. Also here there was an expectation that the HR function could contribute. The main strategic focus in this example has been on multi-skilling. It was assumed that by making every front-line person able to sell and to handle issues around a wide range of products, each will contribute to the process of explaining to existing customers that they can and should bring a larger proportion of their business into this organization. It was also assumed that creating a performance-oriented culture will facilitate this type of cross selling (50%). Once again, by setting this type of target, by providing focused feedback on performance and by rewarding cross selling and improved customer relations, it should be possible to facilitate this organizational strategy.

This example of a strategy contribution matrix and how it can crystallize the strategic contribution of HR is presented here in a simplified form to facilitate understanding. In your organization you should be able to identify more than three strategic areas for focusing medium- to long-term efforts, and thereby more than three HR strategies to make them possible. The basic principle, however, should be the same. The business strategies are the focal points for the strategic efforts of your HR function and it is essential that day-to-day activities do not divert effort from what is required for medium- to long-term success.

The purpose of this contribution matrix is to ensure that everyone involved, both our line customers and internally to the function, understands the basic principles behind our actions and can see how these principles contribute directly to the strategic direction of the organization as a whole. We fill in the matrix by agreeing on the relative percentage contribution of each HR strategy to one or more of the organization's strategies. In this way we can explain to the management team our potential contribution as we see it and make sure that our customers agree with us. In some cases this agreement will be very similar to the one we have already achieved through collecting more detailed customer feedback on each individual HR service as described in earlier chapters. But in many cases, we will find that this process will bring about somewhat different initiatives; the focus here is not on improving the quality, effectiveness and efficiency of each service that we provide, but on specifying what we can do to help people guide the organization towards the achievement of its long-term strategic vision, one that may be dramatically different from the current situation. This does not mean that we stop providing all existing services. Though this contribution matrix, everyone should begin to understand how the long-term transformation of the organization will gradually shift our direction, rather like the way one gradually navigates a large ship. In the short term, the change in the ship's direction may be almost imperceptible, but in the long term, the ship may be turned completely to face a new direction.

Once we have completed the strategy contribution matrix we need to use our own strategies to guide the objectives that we set for each of the HR management services for which we are responsible. Once again, the simplest way of ensuring that we are clear about our plans is to develop an activity contribution matrix. An example of this type of approach for Training services is illustrated in Figure 6.2.

This training activity contribution matrix describes a number of specific training initiatives and how they contribute to the high-level HR strategies identified earlier in this chapter. By specifying this type of contribution we can identify strategic activities and distinguish them from other more routine training services. This analysis makes it possible to review all current activities and decide how best to invest the organization's resources in achieving its medium- to long-term aims. Non-strategic activities may be very important as well, but this analysis can provide a more systematic process for reviewing what is being done and for determining priorities.

The activity contribution matrix enables us to see how each service we provide helps to achieve the overall HR strategy. By relating activities to the organization's overall strategy through the strategic contribution

FIGURE 6.2 Human Resource activity contribution matrix

Training activities	Delayer and empower	Create multi-skilling	Develop a performance-oriented culture	Total
Cross train front office staff to handle all product areas	20%	80%		100%
Implement performance management training for all supervisory staff	20%		80%	100%
Establish basic training for all staff in how to act in an empowered way, including limitations (e.g. how to seek an authorization)	80%		20%	100%

matrix, we can trace the contribution of each of our HR activities to the organization's overall success. This may also enable us to show how the entire budget of our function is linked to the achievement of overall organizational success. We can then become much clearer about the focus for each one of our activities; for example, the provision of training is not a process in its own right. This contribution matrix enables us to decide on the priorities in training content and the process we need to provide to support the overall strategic aims of the function and of the organization as a whole. Such a strategic analysis is very different from what we have done in previous chapters. In this case we base our priorities on their contribution to the long-term business strategies. Previously we used our own self-assessments and feedback from our internal clients as a basis for determining priorities. In some cases the results will be very similar. In many other organizations, however, the two types of analysis will produce very different results. Line management clients will provide us with feedback about how we can best satisfy their own short-term needs. These needs will not always be based on strategic business requirements since they will tend to be operational. Strategic business requirements will usually involve large-scale organizational change and our current line manager clients will also be subject to these changes. It is therefore important to distinguish between what we need to do to satisfy short-term operational requirements and what we need to do to contribute to the strategic business requirements.

One set of guidelines is no more important than the other. As a function we need to be aware of both and to balance our available resources accordingly. The key in both cases is to solicit organizational support for the way in which we divide our resources. Our middle management clients should be engaged in establishing a common set of operational priorities for HR service activities. Usually, the senior management team will be our strategic client with whom we should agree on the amount of investment required to support medium- and long-term initiatives that the business as a whole needs in order to implement its strategic initiatives successfully.

CHAPTER SEVEN

Setting hard and soft targets for Human Resource service delivery

This chapter describes a process for specifying targets for HR services. We explain the difference between hard and soft targets and show how they apply to various types of services.

In most organizations the HR function provides a wide array of services to internal clients. Most of these services, however, do not have a clear definition of targets, nor are they related to the overall strategy for the function or for the organization. If we do not have clear targets it becomes impossible to monitor and evaluate our effectiveness and it is very difficult to improve. Therefore, once we have used the processes described in the previous chapters to establish priorities for our current and future activities, it becomes possible to specify clear targets for each HR service.

The targets we set must relate to each service so that we can measure its effectiveness. Different types of target should apply to almost any service provision. The most basic type of target focuses on implementing new services or new components to existing services. This can be called a milestone target and relates to a function, and/or a job holder responsible for it, which or who will implement something new by a given date and according to plan. This target is not really related to the provision of an ongoing service but rather to setting up new initiatives. An example of a milestone target in training services could aim to develop a training programme for front office staff that will provide them with the skills required for cross product selling.

Once we have established a given service, however, it becomes necessary to set specific targets to ensure that the service is provided efficiently and effectively. The first type of target for measurings ongoing service provision usually has to do with direct and indirect costs. What it costs us to provide any service may relate both to the budgetary sums as well as to staff time involved in the provision of service, which in turn can be related to their cost of employment. Costs would also involve facilities used in service provision and there are other administrative costs that have an indirect impact on the provision of services internally. In many cases the costs will have come directly from the budget as we have seen in Chapter Six, which discussed activity analysis. For the training example described above, a cost target could be to provide cross-product training to all new staff at no more than £200 per person excluding their time costs but including all direct costs (e.g. facilities and materials used).

In addition to cost, probably the most important type of target relates to the quality of services. Our service quality has to be defined as the degree to which what we provide is what our customers want. This can be related to information provided earlier regarding feedback from internal customers about the importance of each of the services we provide and their quality. We can also measure service quality at the point of delivery by, for example, soliciting feedback from managers and candidates after training. A sample target of this type can aim to achieve average satisfaction ratings of at least four on a five-point scale in feedback questionnaires administered to new staff and their supervisors following the cross-product training.

In addition to the question of what we provide, there is a subset of targets that should relate to how we provide it. Do we provide services in a way that is easy for our internal customers to consume? The third component of quality relates to when we provide the service, that is, to its timeliness. An example here could read: Ensure that all new staff complete the cross-product training no later than one month after they join and that remedial work for those who do not pass the end-of-programme competence test is provided within the following week.

By combining the what, how, when and for how much criteria we should be able to set effective targets for each of the services provided by the HR function.

In rare cases there might also be revenue targets related to service provision. This is a new trend where organizations attempt to assign internal costs and require our client population to budget for services they buy from us. This may be part of an attempt to enable line managers to buy services not only from within the organization but also externally. The assumption may be that this internal market will facilitate the effectiveness and efficiency of service provision. To the degree that there are internal cost allocations we may want to set revenue targets on services. In many cases training and recruitment are probably the key service where revenue targets are applicable but other services may gradually migrate towards them as the function moves towards a consultancy model charging for services daily and/or as more HR services are outsourced by the organization to external providers. A revenue target could read as follows: work with Operations to ensure that they budget for cross-product training and that they use our services to provide at least 75% of programmes with a 'profit' of 15% over our internal costs including our overhead allocations.

In setting milestone, cost, quality and maybe even revenue targets, the focus is usually on a combination of quantitative and qualitative targets. It is important to have quantitative targets where we can use numbers to specify costs and even quality targets as gathered from ratings of customer satisfaction on the delivery of service. But it is usually critical not only to assign a quantitative target but also to have more high-level qualitative targets related to each HR service. In many cases the numbers do not necessarily reflect what is really important and we may want to have more qualitative measures about feedback from customers that will be more meaningful in the long-term.

In establishing targets it is possible to go to extremes and identify a large numbers of targets for each sub-service and so end up with hundreds of targets to describe a service or the range of services provided by the HR function. This approach may seem quasi-scientific but, in reality, a large number of targets makes it impossible to monitor the effectiveness and efficiency of service provision. This approach will require everyone to spend endless hours specifying targets and changing them as internal requirements change, thereby using up time and resources better spent in service delivery.

It is usually better to have two or three targets assigned to every service rather than to try to measure absolutely everything. You will find that by prioritizing the targets some of the key things will give a good enough understanding of the quality of service provision and, therefore, will provide a much better basis for improvement. The improvement processes themselves may require additional measurements but these will evolve as a result of team efforts to assess service delivery. The main point is to focus everyone's attention on a small number of key items to concentrate efforts on significant improvement opportunities. In general, therefore, you should probably have around seven to ten targets for each person in the HR function, thereby focusing everyone's attention on the key outcomes that will ensure the overall effectiveness of the function.

It is important to emphasize the point about differentiating between milestone targets and the various types of outcome target described above. In many cases it is tempting to establish milestone targets instead of those which evaluate the quality of the outcomes once the service is being provided.

On their first attempt, therefore, many practitioners will concentrate on implementing a course by a certain date, or getting a certain number of people on the course, rather than focusing on the target itself, which is the result of people attending the course. In many cases it is difficult to provide quantitative measures of the long-term effectiveness of participation in courses. However, it is much better to have even a simple measurement of perceived long-term satisfaction from the content and process of training or to measure managers' satisfaction from the fact that they saw some benefit from their staff attending the course, than just to measure numbers of people attending or the implementation of courses on time.

Milestone targets are usually important when one is establishing a new service as part of regular project management processes. But measuring the effectiveness and efficiency of service provision should go beyond milestone targets into attempting to describe, even in qualitative terms, the match between actual and expected outcomes of service provision.

Setting targets is one of the first steps in improving the delivery of service by the HR function. It is, therefore, very important that target setting is done by the people who are responsible for the provision of the service itself. By thinking about each HR service in relation to key milestones, quality, cost and maybe revenue that should be achieved, those who are involved in service provision have an opportunity to rethink what they are doing and to make sure that their actions are related directly to contributing to the organization as a whole. Usually this target-setting process is best achieved by asking groups of staff who are responsible for service provision to establish how they could measure the effectiveness of the service for which they are responsible. Once they have defined the measurements they can attempt to set targets that represent what it would mean to do a very good job.

In some organizations it has been helpful to establish not only minimum targets but also to define an especially superior service in each area. By doing so the service providers create their own mini vision for the service as it could be if they really succeeded. This process is, therefore, an initial step in the continuous improvement process. By beginning to share a vision of what the service could be like, those staff who participate in service delivery begin to own the need to improve what they are currently doing.

The data collected so far, as described in earlier chapters, can help those responsible for service provision to begin to understand priorities. However, when we get to the setting of targets for an individual service, those responsible for delivery will need to go back to their internal customers to understand in much more detail what they specifically want and how they would assess whether what they were receiving matched their expectations of cost and timelessness. This process may benefit in some cases from a more formalized approach through Service Level Agreements (SLA), which a number of organizations have began to implement in their HR area. An SLA is a more formal agreement with an internal client to deliver an HR service within specified standards of cost and quality. This should simulate the type of agreement one would have with an external supplier and is designed to ensure that the internal supplier, in this case the HR function, acts in a commercially effective manner. What is important here is not to attempt the impossible by describing each service in ultimate detail as this could involve undesirable bureaucracy; the people involved in service delivery and their customers would then spend more time defining the service than delivering it.

As described earlier, the key for effective service delivery is to focus on the three or four most important elements and to describe them in a way that may be qualitative but is clear to those receiving and those delivering the service. In general, this type of discussion with one's customers will clarify what is important. It will also identify things which the HR function as a 'supplier' may think are important, but that actually may be less critical to their internal customers – they should be the ones that define the key criteria for effective and efficient services in the organization.

It is usually relevant to refer back periodically to the activity contribution matrix described in Chapter Six, and sometimes to the strategy contribution matrix, to ensure that our current targets and actions clearly relate to the overall strategic direction of the function and the organization.

The final very important point in understanding the process of target setting is the need for realism. It is very easy to establish targets that are far removed from the current delivery of services within the organization but this will only end in disillusionment both for the provider and the intended recipient. Therefore, one always needs to keep in mind that change has to occur one step at a time and that it is more effective to set a sequence of targets that establish expectations this year and next year. The staff who provide the service and their customers can then see a continuous improvement process where everyone is involved in achieving the overall long-term goal. The key is to ensure that customers and internal suppliers work as a team to make sure the organization improves because internal services improve. This is far better than creating adversarial situations where contracts have to be adhered to, or negative consequences will occur.

Once targets are set, it may be possible also to benchmark across organizational settings. People within the service delivery teams may volunteer to call other organizations to compare a number of key targets. For example, when focusing on recruitment, some targets may relate to the overall cost of recruitment and to the time from the moment a requirement has been established to when a candidate or a shortlist of candidates has been identified. Obviously these would vary greatly according to the level of the job, the location and the nature of the industry. Therefore, any benchmarking information from other organizations has to be taken with a lot of scepticism rather than seen as a hard target that must be achieved. But by gaining some understanding of other organizations' practices, it may be possible to identify priority areas for improvement. An easier and usually more effective benchmarking process is to compare performance in one business unit to the performance in another business unit within the same organization. This type of comparison is usually easier because it is simpler to get access to the relevant information and because the similarity of terms used within a single business makes it much easier to compare like with like.

The key here, as in all previous efforts, is to ensure that everyone participates in the process, both in the part of the team providing the service and the key internal customers. This will ensure understanding of the difficulties involved and also of where everyone is trying to get to to ensure the medium- and long-term success of the organization. The simple form in Figure 7.1 could be used to record and monitor the targets assigned to each person in the HR function.

As mentioned earlier, it is usually best to ask each manager responsible for an HR service to complete this form. Managers should be encouraged to involve their staff in defining the required levels of achievement and to work very closely with their internal customers to ensure that these objectives meet their needs.

Finally, the complete set of objectives that describe the total HR function should be circulated to prevent duplication and/or gaps. This process of service definition within the HR function and through interaction with internal customers will be the best way to ensure that everyone is working together towards the achievement of a common set of objectives.

FIGURE 7.1 A form for recording and monitoring targets

Objectives for the year				
Name		Title		Date completed
Objective	On target performance	Exceptional performance	Rating	Comments on actual performance
Implement cross product training for all front office staff	1 Cost of £200 per head 2 Within one week of joining 3 Feedback rating of 4 on 5-point scale	1 Cost of £150 per head (by using self-instructional materials) 2 Within two weeks of joining 3 Feedback rating of 4 on 5-point scale		

CHAPTER EIGHT

Improving the Human Resource function

This chapter focuses on what should be done to ensure an effective process leading towards the improvement of the HR function. Effectively planning, implementing and monitoring this organization change process will ensure that we achieve the desired results.

The most important ingredient for improving any service is ownership. Only those who are actually responsible for delivering a service can improve its quality. They are the only ones who really understand what is being done and who can change what they are doing in a meaningful way to improve their effectiveness and efficiency.

It is, therefore, impossible to improve the quality of service by issuing orders, or through establishing an audit process by senior managers or external consultants and then trying to enforce the findings and recommendations onto the team responsible for the day-to-day provision of the service. It is true that change needs leadership and that those who provide the service usually do not see the need for change without the leadership who provide that type of vision. But the most effective leadership will achieve true change only through inspiring those who provide the service to clients.

More specifically, the only way that services can be improved is by trying to generate commitment on the part of the service delivery team to interact more closely with the receivers of the services who, in the case of the HR function, are their internal customers. Only by understanding who are the key customers involved, what they want and how both teams (of clients and their suppliers) can work together to improve service provision in the interest of the entire organization, will the HR function be able to achieve a sound foundation for realistic service improvement.

Managerial attempts to put pressure on staff in order to achieve new targets overnight may bring about small changes in the short term, but in the long term will usually not result in any real change.

Therefore, improving any one of the services provided by the HR function must start with encouraging the key participants in the service provision team to acknowledge the need for improvement. This is usually best achieved by getting them to own a process of diagnosis as the first step in a longer improvement process. It is, therefore, the staff who provide the day-to-day service who should be responsible for collecting all the data described in previous chapters. By summarizing all that information and using it to conduct a SWOT (Strengths, Weaknesses, Opportunities and Threats) analysis, that is, the strengths and weaknesses of the current services and the opportunities for improvement as well as the threats to the function and the organization if the service is not improved. An example of a SWOT analysis is provided in Figure 8.1.

The SWOT analysis can help the function agree on what has to be changed and why. It is important, however, to remember that almost any service provided within an organization is highly dependent on other services provided in it. This means that one step will be part of a larger chain within the service delivery process and that changing the nature of any one of the steps in the service will cause a reaction in the other service components provided.

For example, if we change the way pay relates to performance it will have a major impact on all the other HR services. Similarly, if we change the responsibility for training from being an organizational responsibility

FIGURE 8.1   A Human Resources SWOT analysis

Strengths	Weaknesses
1 Some staff with HR expertise and good interpersonal skills	1 Still too many admin-oriented HR staff
2 Positive attitude of new MD and line feedback on HR issues (e.g. importance ratings)	2 We think that we provide a better service than line managers think
3 Sufficient budget for innovation	3 Much of our budget is in low priority areas

Opportunities	Threats
1 Survey enables us to agree service levels with line	1 Need to be seen to act quickly or else
2 Staff interest in training can be capitalized on	2 A few strategic business changes will need a lot of expert HR support or they will fail
3 External market good for recruiting a few more HR professionals in priority areas	3 Line managers cannot slow pace of change until some of our people get better trained

to one where the individuals are responsible for their own self development, this will affect other processes within the organization that require staff to be adequately trained in order to perform effectively.

Therefore, once the team of service providers have identified what they see as the key opportunities and threats based on the strengths and weaknesses of a given functional organization, it is important to gather a larger team to review what should and could be done.

That team should ideally include representatives of:

- key customers for the service

- the team who are responsible for service provision

- sometimes, those who may have an indirect relationship to this process (e.g. Finance).

This team needs to agree with the diagnostic SWOT analysis as well as with the new target-setting process that has to be established for a given service. We have already described the key requirements for setting targets, which, as stated earlier, is in itself a part of the improvement process. By ensuring that everyone involved in delivering and receiving services sets a sequence of targets that provide realistic achievable points for improvements that can be implemented this year, next year and the year after, it will be possible to create a shared vision about the service and its contribution to the function and the organization as a whole.

Once the outcome targets have been set, it is important for the team, on the basis of the SWOT analysis, to move into project planning. Where there are large-scale changes, it may be realistic to put together a plan for the change based on project planning procedures, which should already be established in the organization. But usually, when service improvement is initiated, the changes are much more specific and a full project plan may not be required. It is always, however, essential not only to establish the long-term targets but also to set milestones for what will be implemented, by when, in order to ensure that the changes occur.

A simplified service improvement plan could look like the example in Figure 8.2.

Once the SWOT analysis and target setting have been achieved, it is important to assign responsibilities clearly. Responsibilities in some cases may lie with teams, such as the service delivery team, but they are often broken down further into individual responsibilities. Everyone needs to leave the service delivery team meetings and the joint supplier and customer meetings with a clear understanding of what they themselves have to deliver by when.

FIGURE 8.2   An example of a service improvement plan

Improving the provision of training to front office staff high level project plan							
Key step	Responsibility	Week 1	Week 2	Week 3	Week 4	Week 5	Week 6
Agree project plans		XXX					
Collect feedback from internal clients		XXX	XXX				
Present results and agree SWOT analysis				XXX			
Managers' input on new service objectives				XXX			
Complete 1st draft of HR service objectives					XXX		
Solicit feedback from senior management team					XXX	XXX	
Finalize objectives and implementation plan						XXX	
Develop new training materials required for relaunch							Start here
Sell new concept of training to front office supervisors							XXX
Develop monitoring process to assess quality/cost							Within one month

The result of the first steps in the process of service improvements will, therefore, be a high-level plan, which clarifies the strengths and weaknesses of the current service, the opportunities for improvement, the threats if there is no improvement, what needs to be done to change the service in the short, medium and long term, and who is responsible for each component.

All this information should be discussed at a relatively high level because it is easy to spend the year planning rather than to put that effort into actually improving the service. It is important to ensure that there is an effective plan but between three to four team meetings should be sufficient to come up with a plan robust enough to guide long-term action. It is important to remember that the best of plans will have to be changed as a result of numerous internal and external changes and that it is, therefore, better to get it 80% right and to move forward rather than to attempt to get a perfect plan that then requires a large number of meetings every time a small change occurs in the function or in the organization.

The development of a change programme by the service delivery team in conjunction with its key customers paves the way to implementing ways of monitoring service effectiveness within the function. If everyone involved knows that the key milestones of service improvement will be monitored as part of routine management reviews, those involved in service delivery will ensure that these milestones are achieved. The typical barrier to service improvement is the routine provision of the service in its current state. Available resources are committed to the day-to-day routine and even if everyone wants to follow the service improvement plan they are too busy with business as usual.

The only way to ensure that the plan is implemented, therefore, is to ensure that everyone knows that achievement versus the milestones in the plan is going to be reviewed at senior management level and that real consequences will be attached to non-achievement of the plan. This task is much easier when specific responsibilities for change have been well assigned, since there is then an incentive to ensure that these changes happen.

In addition to the need for widespread involvement, for detailed planning and for continuous monitoring of progress, it is essential to ensure effective communication. Everyone involved directly and indirectly in providing and in receiving the service will develop their own picture of what is and is not happening in relation to their expectations. We should, therefore, not merely implement the planned changes in service delivery, but must attempt to ensure that everyone is aware of what will be changing by when and for what reasons. Otherwise the audience, who are not directly involved in implementation, will judge what they see according to their own frame of reference. They may see some actions as part of a wider 'plot' to reduce their power or as a sign of the function's inability to address their needs.

Effective implementation will require, therefore, not only wide-scale involvement in the planning phase, but also continuous communication with a wide audience about the changes being implemented. This communication should be two-way; those who have direct experience of the changes should let the service providers know if they are being unrealistically implemented and whether the original plans need to be adjusted.

Some actions that seem effective at the planning stage will become problematic when implemented. This is usually because the inter-relationships between different organizational processes become apparent only when we are trying to change something. Only at that point will other service providers realize that the planned changes interfere with something they are responsible for. By ensuring two-way communication, it will be possible to incorporate such new input into a revised plan that will ensure that the service improvements fit well within the rest of the relevant processes operating in the organization.

The following example illustrates the change management approach described here:

One of the key priorities for service improvement in our case study organization was to develop and implement an effective performance management process with specific integrated business targets for teams and individuals. This process would also include an effective personal development process that ensures that individuals' and teams' strengths and weaknesses are identified and addressed in time to support strategic business requirements.

An integrated team of HR practitioners with different areas of expertise (e.g. development, training, pay, IR) was put together with a number of line managers and staff to ensure that the implementation plan addressed requirements but was also usable from the clients' point of view. The agreed plan, with its milestones for implementation, was reviewed regularly by the top management team to see who was completing what phase of the plan and to review feedback from early users to ensure that those plans were adjusted to fit the experience of implementation.

This feedback was a result of regular communication meetings with other HR staff and with line managers who commented on the new processes and their usefulness. These communication sessions were led by the combined implementation team of HR and line managers so that everyone involved was clear about the joint ownership and the new process was not seen as 'another good idea from Personnel'.

The key ingredient for this, as well as most other efforts at organizational change, was the concept of the ripple effect. Instead of succumbing to the usual temptation for implementing a new process across the entire organization as part of a massive change management project, this team understood that it is more effective to do things gradually. Any change is difficult for those involved even if they think it is a good idea. After all, how many of us would like to eat less, exercise more and change our balance of priorities between work and fun? But it is very difficult to change the way we are used to behaving.

In an organizational setting, change is even more difficult, since there are many players who may disagree with the need for change and/or who may feel that change will threaten their current position within the power structure. Therefore, to introduce even the most logical organizational change, one is faced not only with the inertia of current behaviour but also with the active opposition of those who feel, rightly or wrongly, that they are better off without it.

The ripple effect change management strategy is based on an attempt to minimize the power of the opposition in direct proportion to the degree to which the new processes become embedded into the organization. The original plan should not, therefore, focus on changing everyone's behaviour but on changing the behaviour of a few key players who can be counted on to support the new initiative. After these players have been successful and after we have incorporated their feedback comments into the plans for service improvement, we can then progress to the next wave of change implementers, and so on.

Assuming that the proposed change does improve organizational effectiveness we will find that this change management strategy will gradually ensure that we do not need to sell the change. More and more internal clients will want to join the bandwagon and use our revised process to improve their effectiveness. There will always be a hard core of resisters but their power can be challenged towards the end when we can demonstrate widespread support from satisfied internal customers.

In this case study organization it was possible to implement the new performance management process first in one part of the organization, use that experience for introducing minor changes in the proposed process and then gradually to expand across one division after the other. Every month there was a steering group meeting that included, in addition to the HR managers responsible for implementation, three managers representing internal customers. This team reviewed the feedback from the field and made sure that required changes were introduced along the way.

Finally, the whole project plan was initially communicated through the staff newsletter so that everyone knew what was going to happen. A progress report was also printed half way through, including positive feedback from the division that was first to implement the new process.

This made it possible to create a positive impression of the changes and thereby to help the successful implementation of the next stages in the project plan.

The final point of consideration in planning and implementing changes in the provision of HR services concerns the internal resistance of some of our own staff. If we are really trying to implement fundamental changes to the philosophy of our function and its direct contribution to improving business effectiveness, we are very likely to find a great deal of more or less overt resistance from within the function. This could take the form of prolonged discussions on 'best practice', of passive participation that has no follow-up action or of external support which hides behind-the-scenes political efforts to subvert the process of real change. Even though it is easy to understand how difficult it is for anyone to change their behaviour significantly, this type of internal resistance is the most difficult to handle. The external task is hard enough without having to worry about the support of those who are behind you. There are no simple answers for dealing with internal resistance other than to know that it is there and that if you do not see it, then you are either not trying to change things in a fundamental manner, or you are blind to key internal processes.

Everything that has been mentioned so far in this chapter should support the effort to ensure staff commitment to the process of change. Participating in the diagnostic process, contributing to plans for change, having specific responsibilities for parts of the implementation, being aware of the ongoing monitoring process and taking part in two-way communication about what is being implemented and how it can be improved, will facilitate getting more staff on board. But as with the internal clients, there will remain a hard core who will be waiting for the changes to go away and/or will be resisting them more actively. The process of gradual implementation described earlier will make it possible to delay dealing with resistance until you are more secure in the planned process of change. But internally it may be necessary to make some early visible movements to demonstrate that the change will happen and that input is required to ensure effectiveness rather than to examine the fundamental need for change. Reducing the power of those who oppose the changes and increasing the power of those who support it should be viewed as part of the process of implementation and should, therefore, be subject to in-depth consideration. It may be advantageous to change the internal organization of the function early in the process of change but effective communication will be the key to success. Those responsible for the management of change need to control the process of communication both inside the function and among your clients. This will ensure that key managers and staff understand why you are changing certain players and that they feel that you have consulted them in advance to ensure that their views and support are available.

And one last point that cannot be avoided. It would be very rare for you to succeed in implementing fundamental change with existing management and staff. Both resistance and lack of competence will almost always make it necessary to change some key players in your team.

Figure 8.3 summarizes the key stages in the process of improving the effectiveness of HR services.

FIGURE 8.3   Key stages in improving HR services

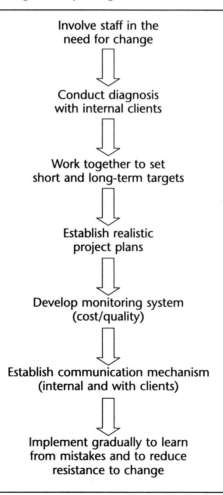

Involve staff in the
need for change

Conduct diagnosis
with internal clients

Work together to set
short and long-term targets

Establish realistic
project plans

Develop monitoring system
(cost/quality)

Establish communication mechanism
(internal and with clients)

Implement gradually to learn
from mistakes and to reduce
resistance to change

CHAPTER NINE

Conclusions

To summarize, this book was designed to support a process for improving the effectiveness of the HR function. A wide array of research results and specific data collection tools have been provided to enable HR practitioners to collect diagnostic information about current strengths in service delivery and about priority areas for improvement.

This diagnostic data was then intended to be used as part of a process of establishing a revised HR strategy for the function directly tied to the overall strategy of the organization. The specification of such a functional strategy should then become a foundation for identifying service targets and setting milestones for implementing service improvements. Finally, developing a highly participative planning process, monitoring the implementation of change, communicating with all those involved in the provision and reception of service changes and handling resistance from clients and from your own staff, are all key components of effective change management required for the successful improvement of HR services to increase their added value to the achievement of the business strategy.

The benchmark data provided here should enable you to compare where you are with other HR functions. But implementing service improvements is a long-term process and any type of emotional and professional support will be of great help. I would encourage you, therefore, to develop a network with other HR practitioners who are trying to improve the effectiveness of their function. This leadership role is a lonely one and by discussing successes and failures with others, more informally in professional meetings or more formally through engaging the services of senior consultants who can provide a general sounding board (rather than implement specific solutions), you will be able to test your ideas and discuss alternative approaches for handling the inevitable barriers to success. Collaboration across organizational boundaries will help you to implement changes more effectively and learn from each other's experience.

The Appendix provides you with copies of all the data collection and analysis tools used in this book. Adapting these tools for your needs should provide you with the basic foundation for successfully changing the provision of HR services in your organization.

Appendix

1   **A model for improving the contribution of the HR function**
     (see Figure 1.5)

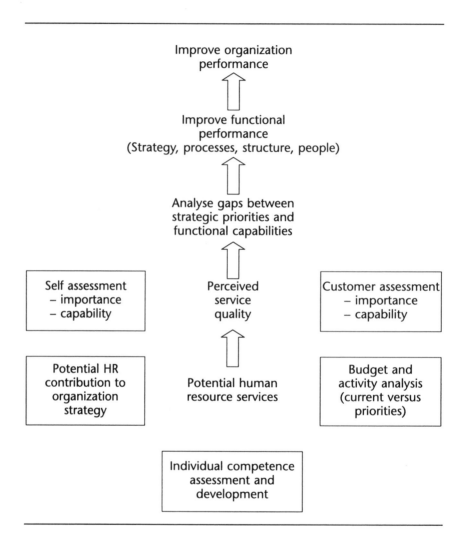

2 The range of services provided by the HR function
(see Figure 2.1)

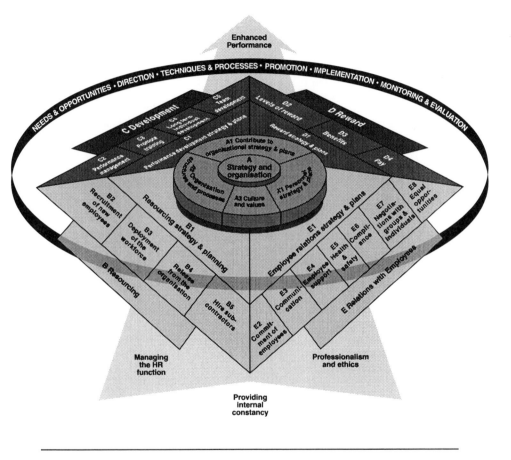

3   A questionnaire for assessing the importance of HR services and the current level at which they are provided
(see Chapter 2)

The key functions of personnel

Listed below are Personnel services grouped under five headings. Under each function we would like you to respond to the following:

■   **Importance for the future success of your organization**
Please circle the number in the column that best reflects the importance of each function to the future success of your organization.

■   **Current personnel capability**
The capability of your Personnel function to deliver each Personnel function effectively.

Please circle the number in the column that best reflects the current capability of your organization to perform this function.

You have the opportunity to comment on your ratings if you wish.

A. Strategy and organization	Importance for future success 1 Critical 2 Very important 3 Important 4 Helpful 5 Not important					Current personnel capability 1 Exceptionally good 2 Very good 3 Good 4 Fair 5 Poor				
Contribute to the overall strategy of the organization by providing generalist and specialist information and advice	1	2	3	4	5	1	2	3	4	5
Develop and maintain an appropriate personnel strategy to support the overall strategy of the organization	1	2	3	4	5	1	2	3	4	5
Enable the creation of an organization structure and work processes that maximize the performance of people at work	1	2	3	4	5	1	2	3	4	5
Facilitate the development of organizational values and culture required to support its strategy	1	2	3	4	5	1	2	3	4	5
Facilitate external relations (e.g. purchasers, local authorities, educational institutions)	1	2	3	4	5	1	2	3	4	5

Comments: _____

_____

_____

B. Resourcing	Importance for future success 1 Critical 2 Very important 3 Important 4 Helpful 5 Not important					Current personnel capability 1 Exceptionally good 2 Very good 3 Good 4 Fair 5 Poor				
Develop and maintain workforce planning to support current and future requirements	1	2	3	4	5	1	2	3	4	5
Recruit and select people into the organization	1	2	3	4	5	1	2	3	4	5
Optimize the deployment of staff within the organization	1	2	3	4	5	1	2	3	4	5
Identify individual potential to develop and meet future resourcing requirements	1	2	3	4	5	1	2	3	4	5
Release people from the organization (e.g. retirement, redundancy)	1	2	3	4	5	1	2	3	4	5
Engage non-core and temporary staff	1	2	3	4	5	1	2	3	4	5

Comments:_____

_____

_____

C. Development										
Establish and maintain performance management	1	2	3	4	5	1	2	3	4	5
Establish opportunities to enhance individual capability (e.g. training)	1	2	3	4	5	1	2	3	4	5
Promote longer-term individual development processes	1	2	3	4	5	1	2	3	4	5
Facilitate team development processes	1	2	3	4	5	1	2	3	4	5

Comments:_____

_____

_____

D. Compensation and benefits										
Develop and maintain a reward strategy (e.g. pay, benefits)	1	2	3	4	5	1	2	3	4	5
Establish and maintain the criteria for ensuring appropriate level of reward	1	2	3	4	5	1	2	3	4	5
Implement and maintain processes to define employees' terms and conditions of employment	1	2	3	4	5	1	2	3	4	5
Pay contracted employees and others	1	2	3	4	5	1	2	3	4	5
Administer benefits and other payments	1	2	3	4	5	1	2	3	4	5

Comments:_____

_____

_____

E. Relations with employees	Importance for future success 1 Critical 2 Very important 3 Important 4 Helpful 5 Not important					Current personnel capability 1 Exceptionally good 2 Very good 3 Good 4 Fair 5 Poor				
Develop and maintain commitment of employees in times of change (e.g. support change programmes)	1	2	3	4	5	1	2	3	4	5
Promote effective communication within the organization	1	2	3	4	5	1	2	3	4	5
Provide counselling and welfare support for the mutual benefit of the organization and the individual	1	2	3	4	5	1	2	3	4	5
Ensure compliance with Personnel-related legislation and internal policies	1	2	3	4	5	1	2	3	4	5
Provide processes for handling grievances and discipline	1	2	3	4	5	1	2	3	4	5
Consult and/or negotiate with employees and/or their representatives to facilitate achievement of organizational goals	1	2	3	4	5	1	2	3	4	5
Promote and ensure equality of opportunity	1	2	3	4	5	1	2	3	4	5
Establish and maintain processes for ensuring health and safety at work	1	2	3	4	5	1	2	3	4	5

Comments: _____

_____

_____

F. Work processes in service delivery

So far we have presented Personnel services and asked you to indicate if they are currently performed in your organization and their importance to the current and future success of your organization.

We would also like your feedback about importance and capability as they apply to the different work processes involved in providing Personnel services.

Assess needs and opportunities to provide and improve Personnel services	1	2	3	4	5	1	2	3	4	5
Design and select techniques and processes for providing Personnel services	1	2	3	4	5	1	2	3	4	5
Market and promote the advantage of utilizing Personnel services	1	2	3	4	5	1	2	3	4	5
Implement and enable others to implement Personnel services	1	2	3	4	5	1	2	3	4	5
Monitor and evaluate the effectiveness of Personnel services	1	2	3	4	5	1	2	3	4	5

Comments: _____

_____

_____

4   High-level analysis of the HR budget according to services provided
(see Figure 4.1)

Current human resource activities

Activity	Staff		Other costs	
	No.	Cost	Variable	Fixed
		TOTAL		
1. **Strategy and organization**				
1.1 Contribution to organization strategy				
1.2 Organization structure and work processes (changing, improving)				
1.3 Culture and values (defining, changing)				
2. **Resourcing**				
2.1 Recruitment and selection				
2.2 Internal deployment				
2.3 Releasing (redundancy, retirement)				
2.4 Sub-contractors and temporary staff				
3. **Development**				
3.1 Performance management				
3.2 Training				
3.3 Long-term individual development				
3.4 Team development				
4. **Reward**				
4.1 Levels of reward (job evaluation)				
4.2 Paying employees				
4.3 Administering benefits				
5. **Relations with employees**				
5.1 Ensuring employee commitment				
5.2 Internal communication				
5.3 Employee support services (i.e. counselling)				
5.4 Health and Safety				
5.5 Compliance				
5.6 Negotiations with groups and individuals				
5.7 Grievance and discipline				
5.8 Equal opportunities				
6. **Other HR services** (please specify)				
7. **Internal processes**				
7.1 Managing the HR function				
7.2 Internal meetings/co-ordination				
7.3 HR data – input, analysis, presentation				
7.4 Evaluating the effectiveness of HR services				
7.5 Improving existing HR services				
7.6 OTHER INTERNAL PROCESSES (please specify)				

5 **Analysis by each HR staff member of their activity according to the type of service provided** (see Chapter 4)

Current human resource activities

Please indicate below the percentage of time that YOU spend in an average week on each of the following HR areas of service. You may want to refer to the enclosed definitions to assist you in your ratings. Please make sure that the total percentages of your time add up to 100%. Because of the seasonal nature of some of our activities you can indicate variations according to the different seasons. You can complete the first column if such variations do not exist in your work.

Activity	Percent time spent in a given week			
	Jan.–Mar.	April–June	July–Sept.	Oct.–Dec.
1. Strategy and organization				
1.1 Contribution to organization strategy				
1.2 Organization structure and work processes (changing, improving)				
1.3 Culture and values (defining, changing)				
2. Resourcing				
2.1 Recruitment and selection				
2.2 Internal deployment				
2.3 Releasing (redundancy, retirement,)				
2.4 Sub-contractors and temporary staff				
3. Development				
3.1 Performance management				
3.2 Training				
3.3 Long-term individual development				
3.4 Team development				
4. Reward				
4.1 Levels of reward (job evaluation)				
4.2 Paying employees				
4.3 Administering benefits				
5. Relations with employees				
5.1 Ensuring employee commitment				
5.2 Internal communication				
5.3 Employee support services (i.e. counselling)				
5.4 Health and Safety				
5.5 Compliance				
5.6 Negotiations with groups and individuals				
5.7 Grievance and discipline				
5.8 Equal opportunities				
6. Other HR Services (please specify)				
7. Internal processes				
7.1 Managing the HR function				
7.2 Internal meetings/co-ordination				
7.3 HR data – input, analysis, presentation				
7.4 Evaluating the effectiveness of HR services				
7.5 Improving existing HR services				
7.6 OTHER INTERNAL PROCESSES (please specify)				
Total	100%	100%	100%	100%

6   Bar code guide for collecting activity data from HR staff
(see Chapter 4)

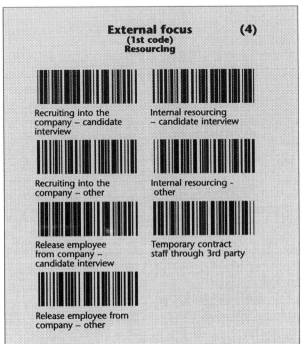

7   **COMPSCAN**
    A questionnaire for assessing the importance of HR skills to each staff member and their current capability
    (see Chapter 5)

PERSONNEL STANDARDS LEAD BODY
COMPSCAN
Competence in Personnel: self assessment

This questionnaire is designed for you and your manager to describe your competence in being able to perform a range of Personnel functions.

It will also enable you to specify where you would like to develop your competence further in this field.

This information will be used to identify priority areas for training and development activities in order to improve the quality of our services to the organization.

Name: _____   Job title: _____

Date: _____

Age: _____   Sex: M ____   F ____   Years of Personnel experience: _____

Role: Managerial _____   Professional _____   Administrative _____

I would describe myself as a Personnel: Generalist _____   Specialist _____

Competency in the key functions of Personnel

Listed below are Personnel functions grouped under five headings. We would like you to rate against each function:

- **Importance for current job**
  Please circle the number in the column that best reflects the importance of that function to your success in your current job. Circle zero if the function is not relevant.
- **Current level of competence**
  Please circle the number in the column that best reflects your level of competence in performing each function. We assume that due to previous experience, you will be competent also in functions that do not form part of your current job responsibilities.
- **Training and development needs**
  Please tick (√) this column if you feel that you would benefit from participating in training and development activities to increase your competence in a given function. Please indicate the specific nature of your requirement in the open-ended section provided after each group of functions.

A. Strategy and organization	Importance for current job 1 Not relevant 2 Small part of 3 Important part of 4 Very important for success 5 Critical for success					Current level of competence 1 Not competent 2 Can do only a little in this area 3 Can do most basic things 4 Can do everything well 5 Am a recognized authority					Training and development need
Contribute to the overall **strategy of the organiz-ation** by providing generalist and specialist information and advice	1	2	3	4	5	1	2	3	4	5	☐
Develop and maintain an appropriate **personnel strategy** to support the overall strategy of the organization	1	2	3	4	5	1	2	3	4	5	☐
Enable the creation of an **organization structure and work processes** that maximize the perform-ance of people at work	1	2	3	4	5	1	2	3	4	5	☐
Facilitate the development of **organization values and culture** required to support its strategy	1	2	3	4	5	1	2	3	4	5	☐

Specific training and development needs:_____

_____

_____

B. Resourcing											
Develop and maintain **workforce planning** to support current and future requirements	1	2	3	4	5	1	2	3	4	5	☐
Recruit and select people into the organization	1	2	3	4	5	1	2	3	4	5	☐
Optimize the **deployment of staff** within the organization	1	2	3	4	5	1	2	3	4	5	☐
Identify **individual potential** to develop and meet future resourcing requirements	1	2	3	4	5	1	2	3	4	5	☐
Release people from the organization (e.g. retirement, redundancy)	1	2	3	4	5	1	2	3	4	5	☐
Engage non-core and temporary staff	1	2	3	4	5	1	2	3	4	5	☐

Specific training and development needs:_____

_____

_____

C. Development	Importance for current job 1 Not relevant 2 Small part of 3 Important part of 4 Very important for success 5 Critical for success					Current level of competence 1 Not competent 2 Can do only a little in this area 3 Can do most basic things 4 Can do everything well 5 Am a recognized authority					Training and development need
Establish and maintain **performance management** processes	1	2	3	4	5	1	2	3	4	5	☐
Establish **training opportunities** to enhance individual competence	1	2	3	4	5	1	2	3	4	5	☐
Promote **longer-term individual development** processes	1	2	3	4	5	1	2	3	4	5	☐
Facilitate **team development** processes	1	2	3	4	5	1	2	3	4	5	☐

Specific training and development needs: _____

_____

_____

D. Reward management											
Develop and maintain a **reward strategy** (e.g. pay, benefits)	1	2	3	4	5	1	2	3	4	5	☐
Establish and maintain the criteria for ensuring appropriate **level of reward** (e.g. job evaluation)	1	2	3	4	5	1	2	3	4	5	☐
Implement and maintain processes to define employees **terms and conditions** of employment	1	2	3	4	5	1	2	3	4	5	☐
Pay contracted employees and others	1	2	3	4	5	1	2	3	4	5	☐
Administer **benefits** and other payments	1	2	3	4	5	1	2	3	4	5	☐

Specific training and development needs: _____

_____

_____

E. Relations with employees	Importance for current job 1 Not relevant 2 Small part of 3 Important part of 4 Very important for success 5 Critical for success					Current level of competence 1 Not competent 2 Can do only a little in this area 3 Can do most basic things 4 Can do everything well 5 Am a recognized authority					Training and development need
Develop and maintain **commitment of employees** in times of change (e.g. support change programmes)	1	2	3	4	5	1	2	3	4	5	☐
Promote effective **communication** within the organization	1	2	3	4	5	1	2	3	4	5	☐
Provide **counselling and welfare** support for the mutual benefit of the organization and the individual	1	2	3	4	5	1	2	3	4	5	☐
Ensure **compliance** with Personnel-related legislation and internal policies	1	2	3	4	5	1	2	3	4	5	☐
Provide processes for handling **grievances and discipline**	1	2	3	4	5	1	2	3	4	5	☐
Consult and/or **negotiate** with employees and/or their representatives to facilitate achievement of organizational goals	1	2	3	4	5	1	2	3	4	5	☐
Promote and ensure **equality of opportunity**	1	2	3	4	5	1	2	3	4	5	☐
Establish and maintain processes for ensuring **health and safety** at work	1	2	3	4	5	1	2	3	4	5	☐

Specific training and development needs:_____
_____
_____

F. Work processes in service delivery

So far we have presented Personnel functions and asked you to indicate their importance for your success in your job and also your level of competence in performing them.

In addition we would like your assessment about importance and your level of competence in performing the following work processes across a range of Personnel functions.

Work processes in service delivery	Importance for current job 1 Not relevant 2 Small part of 3 Important part of 4 Very important for success 5 Critical for success					Current level of competence 1 Not competent 2 Can do only a little in this area 3 Can do most basic things 4 Can do everything well 5 Am a recognized authority					Training and development need
Assess **needs and opportunities** to provide and improve Personnel services	1	2	3	4	5	1	2	3	4	5	☐
Design and select **techniques and processes** for providing Personnel services	1	2	3	4	5	1	2	3	4	5	☐
Market and promote the advantage of utilizing Personnel services	1	2	3	4	5	1	2	3	4	5	☐
Implement and enable others to implement Personnel services											
at a **managerial** level	1	2	3	4	5	1	2	3	4	5	☐
at a **professional** level	1	2	3	4	5	1	2	3	4	5	☐
at an **administrative** level	1	2	3	4	5	1	2	3	4	5	☐
Monitor and evaluate the effectiveness of Personnel services	1	2	3	4	5	1	2	3	4	5	☐

Specific training and development needs: _____
_____
_____

G. General utilization

In general, to what degree do you feel that your current job makes it possible for you to perform to the best of your capability?

☐ 0 – Not at all   ☐ 1 – To a small extent   ☐ 2 – Mostly   ☐ 3 – To a large degree   ☐ 4 – Completely

Comments: _____
_____
_____

8   HR strategic contribution matrix (Example)
   (see Figure 6.1)

Organization Strategy

		Reduce costs	Create close agent relations	Cross sell products	Total
Human Resource Strategy	Delayer and empower	70%	10%	20%	100%
	Create multi-skilling	10%	10%	80%	100%
	Develop performance-oriented culture		50%	50%	100%

9   HR activity contribution matrix (Example)
(see Figure 6.2)

Training activities	Delayer and empower	Create multi-skilling	Develop a performance-oriented culture	Total
Cross train front office staff to handle all product areas	20%	80%		100%
Implement performance management training for all supervisory staff	20%		80%	100%
Establish basic training for all staff in how to act in an empowered way, including limitations (e.g. how to seek an authorization)	80%		20%	100%

10   A form for setting Human Resource objectives
(see Figure 7.1)

Objectives for the year				
Name		Title		Date completed
Objective	On target performance	Exceptional performance	Rating	Comments on actual performance
Implement cross product training for all front office staff	1 Cost of £200 per head 2 Within one week of joining 3 Feedback rating of 4 on 5-point scale	1 Cost of £150 per head (by using self-instructional materials) 2 Within two weeks of joining 3 Feedback rating of 4 on 5-point scale		

11   HR SWOT analysis (Example)
(see Figure 8.1)

Strengths	Weaknesses
1 Some staff with HR expertise and good interpersonal skills 2 Positive attitude of new MD and line feedback on HR issues (e.g. importance ratings) 3 Sufficient budget for innovation	1 Still too many admin-oriented HR staff 2 We think that we provide a better service than line managers think 3 Much of our budget is in low priority areas
Opportunities	**Threats**
1 Survey enables us to agree service levels with line 2 Staff interest in training can be capitalized on 3 External market good for recruiting a few more HR professionals in priority areas	1 Need to be seen to act quickly or else 2 A few strategic business changes will need a lot of expert HR support or they will fail 3 Line managers cannot slow pace of change until some of our people get better trained

12   Sample project management form
(see Figure 8.2)

Improving the provision of training to front office staff high level project plan							
Key step	Responsibility	Week 1	Week 2	Week 3	Week 4	Week 5	Week 6
Agree project plans		XXX					
Collect feedback from internal clients		XXX	XXX				
Present results and agree SWOT analysis				XXX			
Managers' input on new service objectives				XXX			
Complete 1st draft of HR service objectives					XXX		
Solicit feedback from senior management team					XXX	XXX	
Finalize objectives and implementation plan						XXX	
Develop new training materials required for relaunch							Start here
Sell new concept of training to front office supervisors							XXX
Develop monitoring process to assess quality/cost							Within one month

13   A model for improving HR services
(see Figure 8.3)

Involve staff in the
need for change

⇩

Conduct diagnosis
with internal clients

⇩

Work together to set
short and long-term targets

⇩

Establish realistic
project plans

⇩

Develop monitoring system
(cost/quality)

⇩

Establish communication mechanism
(internal and with clients)

⇩

Implement gradually to learn
from mistakes and to reduce
resistance to change

Index